VALUES FOR TOMORROW'S CHILDREN

*An Alternative Future for
Education in the Church*

by

John H. Westerhoff III

The Pilgrim Press
New York

The Pilgrim Press
287 Park Avenue South
New York, New York 10010

to
Barnie, my wife,
and our children—Jill, Jack, and Beth
who, while asking all the embarrassing
questions, provided the incentive to reach
for the insights presented in this book

Contents

Preface

It is hard to believe that it was a decade ago that I penned this "tract for our times," as my friend Bob Lynn named it. A host of letters and conversations from readers have filled the years since. On some matters, I have changed my mind. For example, the creative reform of some church schools has caused me to affirm the possibility of church schooling for some children, youth, and adults. Still, having witnessed numerous creative and effective alternatives to the church school, I am led to believe that my original contentions were justified. Nevertheless, other changes in my mind would include a greater emphasis on children learning the biblical story through the use of the arts, especially by meaningful participation in the worship life of a congregation; a major commitment to adult education with an emphasis on the integration and application of the tradition to personal and social life; and a reexamination and the development of creative alternatives for addressing the personal and faith needs of adolescents.

Through these years, I have refined and expanded my thinking on Christian education. But *Values for Tomorrow's Children* remains foundational to my life and work, and I have chosen this new preface to focus on three concerns thus far untouched: the planning of education in the parish; the relationship of evangelism to education; and the question of how parents can bring up their children in the faith.

Planning for education in the parish, I suggest, begins with people and the tradition, not with organization and program. Our faith places three demands upon us. The tradition needs to be transmitted and acquired in ways that it becomes known, internalized, and can be applied to daily personal and social life. Further, persons bring their own personal, social, physical, emotional, spiritual, and intellectual growth needs. These developmental needs also make legitimate demands upon us. The church touches (and can touch) persons' lives in many diverse ways: to plan for education in the church, to become aware of those places where the church touches the lives of individuals and groups, and to evaluate the quality of that touching in terms of the faith's and the person's needs. If the quality of the touching is significant (whether it be in a choir, committee, group, church school, or corporate worship), the educational needs of that person are being met. If the quality is poor, we need to address the reform of these organizations and programs until the quality can be improved and/or new places developed in which the church can significantly touch persons' lives. Thus program and organization is the last issue and not the first issue to be addressed in planning the educational ministry of the church. In this regard, we need always to remember that the quality is more important than quantity—that two three-day retreats, a week in the summer, or eight four-hour intergenerational events can provide more and better educational time than one hour a week during a school year. Regretfully, if we have one hundred persons in our church and only fifty now attend the church school, we typically attempt to attract the others to the church school or eliminate the church school because everyone is not interested. Why don't we simply acknowledge that the church school is for some, but not for all? Once we have done that, we will be able to develop alternative ways to meet the needs of those for whom this institution is not useful without denying its usefulness for others.

Evangelism is concerned with the proclamation of the gospel, conversion, "new births," or the transformation of perceptions, affections, understandings, and behaviors. Catechesis (education as a pastoral ministry) is concerned with teaching, "growing-up," nurture, or the formation of our perceptions, affections, understandings, and behaviors. Historically the Sunday school in the United States focused on evangelism, church life and worship on catechesis. For example, in North Carolina there are a number of Episcopal churches situated next to mills. Each was built and endowed by the owner of the mill; there is a parish house built for the Sunday school and a church for worship. The owner of the mill, at the turn of the century, required millhands to attend Sunday school with the hope and anticipation that they would be converted to Christian faith over and over again, week by week. It was further expected and anticipated that they would attend worship and thereby be nurtured in the faith over and over again, week by week. It was a natural division of labor and a dual concern. What appears to have occurred (a generalization) is that the evangelical churches continued to emphasize "rebirth" as the focus of the church school while placing little or no emphasis on nurture or growing-up in the faith. Mainstream Protestants, however, changed the focus of Sunday school to nurture, thus creating two serious problems. The first was neglect of the importance of nurture in the life and worship of the congregation and the second was neglect of evangelism within the church. As a result many people have had little to grow-up in. Perhaps the Sunday school is best understood as an agency of evangelism, a place where the gospel can be proclaimed, heard, and responded to in ways appropriate to children, youth, and adults over and over throughout their lives. Similarly, perhaps church life and worship can best be understood as the proper context for our continuing growth in the faith.

Over and over again the most-asked question is: how can I bring up my child to be a Christian? I wish I could answer that question. However, I *cannot* answer it from an educational point of view; I *may not* answer it from a moral point of view. Christian formation and nurture is not a process of manipulation or indoctrination; it is rather a sharing of what one has with another. It is through the interaction of us adults with children that we communicate our faith and thus enable children to their own faith. The only question an adult has the moral right to ask is: how can I be more Christian with my child? That too is a difficult question to answer from an education perspective, but it is at least the right question. For this reason I have come to the conclusion that we must begin with adult education. Until we have converted grown-up adults living faithfully in a community of faith which expresses in every aspect of its corporate life the tradition it professes, neither the transformation nor the formation of children in Christian faith will be possible. This book, therefore, along with others, seeks to make a contribution to adult education. It is not a book of answers; it is a book to initiate learning. Learning is always a painful/joyful process. Each of us has overtime beliefs, attitudes, and behaviors which we have acquired. When these are questioned or when we are presented with an alternative, we are forced into a state of dissonance or conflict. As a result, we strive through reflection to reformulate our own beliefs or attitudes or values. Once that is done, we need a community to help us assimilate our new understandings and ways. And so the process goes on over and over again. It is important for us constantly to examine and to evaluate our own understandings and ways in the light of the tradition and the faith of others, along with the continuing reflection and attempts to reformulate our understandings and ways. This process is part and parcel of the life of the Christian. In one sense then we are always being converted and nurtured day by day. That is, we are always having new starts and growing-up. This book is dedicated to those who desire to enter such a journey in learning.

John H. Westerhoff III
Holy Week 1979
Duke University Divinity School

Introduction
by Robert W. Lynn

Auburn Professor of Religious Education and Church and
Community
Union Theological Seminary, New York City

In this book John Westerhoff renews an honorable tradition in American religious literature. He has written a "tract for the times" at a moment in history when it is sometimes difficult to know where one stands and even more hazardous to assess what is needed "for the times."

It has not always been so. A century ago there would have been nothing unusual about the publication of another tract. The evangelical Protestants of early nineteenth-century America delighted in warfare among the "tractarians." If a man had a conviction—or a "persuasion," as the saying went—he would scrape together a few dollars and publish a pamphlet. Such a tract represented a convenient way of joining an argument and continuing the public debate. There were, for instance, many tracts *for* or *against* the Sunday school. John Westerhoff is trying to ignite that ancient argument once again.

Today the arguments embedded in those pamphlets seem strained and burdened with excessive claims to certitude. The tractarians were often contentious men, eager to pick a fight. Yet in the luxury of retrospect, one can respect them. They *cared* for the truth as they saw it. That same quality is not always evident in the present-day disputes over Christian education. In the last decade there has been little, if any, debate about the coming shape of education in the church. After the disappointing failures of the "renewal" movement in the 1960's there has been a quiet retreat from controversy. Where now, in the broad mainstream of American Protestantism, can one find a deeply felt argument about the next step in Christian education? What is the contemporary equivalent of the argument over "conversion" in Sunday school circles during the nineteenth or early twentieth century? It has been years since we have witnessed anything as exciting as the direct clash between the proponents of progressive religious education and their neo-orthodox critics. Instead, the current tendency is to lower our voices to a whimper. What comes through is a muted cry of resignation.

John Westerhoff does not willingly accede to such faint-heartedness. Here is a person who speaks out of his own "persuasion" and so addresses us as persons capable of caring about faithfulness in the educational work of the church. Here, then, is a tract written in the idiom of our time. *Values for Tomorrow's Children* is actually a "scenario," a sketch of one man's anticipation of a *possible* future. Mr. Westerhoff makes no pretense of having consulted the Delphic oracle about *the* future of Christian education. In that respect he is quite unlike the writers of the earlier tracts. He leaves the work of the astrologer to those among us who are foolhardy enough to predict what lies ahead. The only claim to prescience advanced in this tract is the recognition that the future is, in large part, locked up in the minds and hopes of men right now.

Thus the book is an invitation to examine our own expectations and fears. Even more important, *Values for Tomorrow's Children* calls us to engage in renewed conversation about our present and future responsibilities in Christian education. I am ready to begin in that discussion, for I disagree with some of Mr. Westerhoff's diagnosis and more of his prognosis. But, for the moment at least, that is not important. What is significant is his courage in writing a "tract for the times" and his openness to further debate.

John Westerhoff is a "tractarian" suited to the present era. In an interim time between certainties, he has declared himself.

Is anybody listening? I hope so.

To the Reader

I don't want this to be simply another book. Help me to make it different. Most books are written to present an author's opinion. A reader is expected to ponder the author's words in the hope that he will be persuaded that the author is correct. The author acts and the reader passively accepts or rejects what is given. When the reader is finished, he still has the author's book and some of his own opinions about it. I'd like to change that process.

This book is a personal statement. On the basis of my limited experiences, thoughts and conversations, I have penned my present opinions. They are neither meant to be a lecture nor an academic thesis to be debated by scholars. I want my opinion to be the basis for a conversation with those adults who are concerned about tomorrow's children. A conversation with you! My hope is that my opinions will stimulate and facilitate you to write your own book on an alternative future for education in the church.

So before you read another word, find a pencil. Be prepared to write your thoughts, questions, ideas, opinions and examples in the margins of this book. Whether you agree with my position is secondary. Try not to argue with me; counter my thoughts with your own positive opinions. I want you to be writing your own book as you read mine. The book you write will be the important book.

Let me suggest, then, that you flip through my book and find where you want to begin. There is no special reason to follow the order of my chapters. You may think it best to begin your reading with my chapter 6, 7, or 9. Try it. Begin where you wish. Take the chapters in any order you desire. But after you have finished going through my book, and have gathered all your own notes, find some other people who have done the same. Talk over your ideas; compare and contrast them with theirs. By then my book will be unimportant. It will have served the purpose for which it was written. It will have facilitated the writing of your book.

However, now comes the crucial point. Don't spend a lot of time preparing your words for a printing press. Bring your book to life. Organize those in your church who feel as you do; together give shape and form to your thoughts. Let the world see your book in your lives. That's the test for both of us. If my book of words on an alternative future for education in the church has helped you to write a living book for tomorrow's children, then, and only then, will my time in writing my book and your time in reading it be justified.

I. THE OPEN PRESENT

If our present programs of religious education persist there is reason to believe that tomorrow's children may be denied an experience or understanding of the Christian faith. Yet I do not despair. We are, I believe, approaching what could become a fertile stage in the church's life. The times are pregnant with new possibilities. The joys and pains of births surround us; an alternative future for church education can break through. Why? For many and diverse reasons. A few: persons are becoming increasingly disillusioned with our present attempts at education in the church. New issues, problems, and opportunities confront us; old ways of responding prove inadequate. Experimentation and new models erupt here and there.

Don't misunderstand. I'm not suggesting that a great deal of change has already occurred. But I do sense that church education is ripe for change. That's of importance. It is also the theme and rationale for this book. In the future—it ought to begin now—radical changes will have to be made in the church's educational ministry. I hope that these chapters will free some of us to take the necessary steps in the present so as to build a viable, relevant alternative for the future. A first step is an objective look at our present condition.

Prior to writing this book, I began research for an article on what I believed was the ferment in church education. It was never written. As I traveled about the country looking for material, I found a few exciting, creative experiments. But no ferment. Nor could I locate amidst the numerous books on church education one whose contents might incite ferment.

While I was struggling with that article, Dr. Yoshio Fukuyama of Pennsylvania State University sent me *A Curriculum Evaluation Report,* his latest study. His results concurred with my most pessimistic suspicions.

Fukuyama's research supported what critics have been saying for many years: churches lack a serious commitment to education. In most cases the minister has an inadequate preparation to offer leadership. With a low priority on teaching, he places church education in the hands of his laymen. Most churches have difficulty securing teachers. Those responsible for the church school feel that they have to settle for anyone who is willing to take the job. Not only are churches reluctant to impose criteria for teacher selection, but they do not offer adequate teacher education or support. While the typical teacher spends very little time in preparation, the churches neglect to provide satisfactory classroom space, small class loads, classroom assistance, or adequate supplies and equipment.

Dr. Fukuyama's study also revealed numerous discrepancies between the priority church members say they give to Christian education and the time, talent, money, and interest allotted. Characteristically, the church's education committees have a narrow understanding of their responsibility. Both they and other members of the church tend to identify Christian education almost exclusively with the church school and the needs of children and youth. He found that the majority of parents assume that the present church school will somehow "do the job" of Christian education.

"Traditionalism" therefore pervades the church and its educational enterprise. Ministers, teachers and parents all reveal a reluctance to depart from the known. They appear unable to understand Christian education as anything but the work of a Sunday church school where adults teach children what they learned in the ways they learned it. Their own childhood experiences seem to make it impossible for them to think of new possibilities. Even those churches which affirm the need for change appear unable to find a viable alternative to the one-hour-a-week Sunday church school with volunteer teachers. The best they seem able to do is turn their school into a two-hour weekday affair. Waiting for someone else to give them a foolproof plan, they usually maintain their familiar ways of doing things.

That isn't all. There is a growing estrangement between professional church educators (in churches, conferences, and national boards) and the constituency of their churches. Most professional church educators seem to agree that we need to experiment with a variety of new models. They are coming to believe that church education is in need of radical reform. The gap, however, between the professional's visions of new possibilities and the churchman's dreams of old securities increases. For half a century numerous professional church educators have been complaining about the Sunday church school and some have predicted its death. Yet it still remains, in part because many parishioners cannot or will not envision an alternative.

Studies since the thirties have come to the same conclusion. The church school, as the primary or sole means of church education, is inadequate. The crisis becomes more severe. Fewer laymen are willing to take responsibility for the Sunday church school. Increasingly, youth abandon Sunday school classes and children are reluctant to attend. Fewer seminary students are interested in being trained as directors or ministers of Christian education. The professional has become frustrated, the layman fearfully confused.

"Traditionalism" in church education will prevail until we begin to explore viable alternatives for the future. The continued criticism of our existing inadequate programs of church education will only cause greater insecurity and result in a backward-looking conservatism among those of us who must make the decision to explore new possibilities. More than critics, we need visionaries to encourage both those of us who desire change and those who are reluctant to change.

This book intends to provide the basis on which together we might build an alternative future for church education. The notion of an alternative future suggests a style for dealing with the present. Too often we conceive of futuristic thinking as making predictions. I do not intend to predict the future. Rather, I hope to introduce a way of talking about the present which will make alternatives to our present condition possible in the future. Of course, in the process, I will take a stand on the nature of one viable alternative. Yet my views will have little significance unless they are placed beside other views. By comparing contrasting visions and differing concrete proposals an alternative future can emerge.

In one sense the only future which exists is the one embodied in the hopes, dreams, expectations, anticipations, and plans of persons today. So it was that when The

American Academy of Arts and Sciences published a report, "Toward the Year 2000," Daniel Bell opened it with these words:

> Time, said St. Augustine, is a threefold present: the present as we experience it, the past as present memory, and the future as a present expectation. By that criterion, the world of the year 2000 has already arrived, for in the decision we make now . . . the future is committed. . . . The future is not an over-arching leap into the distance; it begins in the present.[1]

Today we are on the edge of tomorrow. The future is with us in the present.

This is primarily a book for those who are interested in acting in the present in behalf of the future; its purpose, to incite discussion; its form, a personal proposal for the church's educational mission. I did not choose to write a carefully reasoned and precise scholarly statement. There are others who have done or will do that job. This book is written with an audience of anxious, searching laymen in mind. I assume that they are interested in the future of the church's educational ministry. *Values for Tomorrow's Children: An Alternative Future for Education in the Church* is a tract—nothing more, nothing less.

This book represents my thought at this moment. I expect that my mind will change as I talk with my readers. I believe that together we can discover a direction for the future.

As we begin, it would be well for us to recall that the church was born the moment a community of people recognized in the events that surrounded the life of Jesus of Nazareth the activity of God and the presence of a new historical necessity.

The mission of Jesus was to summon men to become

God's change agents in the world. He gathered a few men about him and called them disciples (learners). He asked that they "follow him," that is, share experiences together. He identified his understanding of life through the telling of parables. He interpreted their experiences in terms that pointed to the activity and reign of God in the events of history. He called those whose lives had been made new in the encounter of the resurrection event to become apostles (witnesses) of the emerging possibility for a new world.

Thus a small pack of ordinary folk became a dynamic community of faith. At the same moment the church began its educational ministry. That ministry can be carried out poorly or well, but it cannot be avoided.

Daily, each person who claims to be a Christian communicates through his words and actions his understanding of the Christian faith. In the same manner the church, as a community and institution, communicates through its corporate life the nature and character of the Christian faith. It is primarily through such means that children and others learn what it means to be a Christian.

But how often have we met people who reject the gospel or are unable to make a genuine decision for or against it because they never had the good news properly communicated to them? How often have we met people who accept what they think is the Christian faith, but never really became Christians, because they too never had the faith truly communicated? The lives of this second group who claim to be the bearers of the gospel make it difficult for others to make an honest decision.

Communicating the good news, i.e., offering children, youth and adults an authentic experience of it, is an essential aspect of the church's educational ministry. This education occurs through the life and actions of the faith community wherever it exists. The church communicates its faith by being the community of faith, by offering to persons an experience of its message.

Yet in order for the church to be this kind of educating community, it must struggle to understand its message; it must engage in that painful attempt to decide what it must be and do so as to faithfully communicate its faith. This process demands time for reflection.

Without a living example, Christian education is all but impossible. "No truth," wrote Horace Bushnell, "is really taught by words or interpreted by intellectual and logical methods. Truth must be lived into meaning before it can be truly known." That's true. But unless Christians sit down and discover what their actions mean, they might communicate a distortion of the gospel.

There are some people in the church today who in their concern for education have become action oriented. They have realized the importance of the experiential aspect of the church's educational ministry. They are emphasizing that important aspect of education because many of us have forgotten it. Nevertheless sometimes they need to be reminded of the necessity for reflection and study.

Why? Because the actions of the faith community are not automatic. They are a result of a serious search for those actions which best express its faith. There are two basic aspects to the gospel: one expressed through words and ideas, and the other lived as the Good News. The words are necessary in order that the living Word might be identified and interpreted, but the words without the living Word are shallow and bare. The keys to all education are experience and interpretation. Education becomes Christian education when both of these occur to a person within the faith community.

One of the early Church Fathers said, "Christianity is not talk." Some days you would think that is all it is. In church education we have been long on talking and short on living. Most of the time we use the proper words; speaking them with the satisfaction of knowing that they have been used for centuries. With words we attempt to describe and interpret the Christian faith. When we utter them we assume that they are understood by others, that they are filled with significance. But words are symbols for experiences. Without the experience they are at best memorized definition without power, at worst non-sense syllables.

For example, Christianity has rightly been characterized as a religion of salvation. Christ is another name for the one who saves. The Christian faith affirms that God has acted, acts, and will act in the lives of men and nations to heal the sick, make whole the disrupted, free those in bondage and liberate those in captivity. The words "salvation" and "saved" are used to identify where that experience is taking place. They are the symbols used to interpret how God calls us to behave in relationship to our neighbor. But have we experienced health, wholeness, freedom and liberation in the church? Do we know what it means to seek those blessings for others? For too many people the words "saved" and "salvation" have negative rather than positive meaning. They do not point to *the* Word at all. I find few churchmen who acknowledge that these words have significance for their lives; few who say that they point to experiences in the church which have changed their lives; few whose behavior reveals that they live in their power.

Church education needs to be about both *the Word*— living experiences persons have in the faith community— and *the words*—how we talk about (in defining and interpreting) those experiences. Church education cannot afford to do anything less than be about the total life of the community of faith. It is difficult to conceive of a solitary Christian. To be a Christian is to be in fellowship with that historic community of faith called the church. To experience and understand the Christian faith is to participate in the life of a contemporary faith community—a congregation, that is, wherever two or three persons gather to make real in their experience the heritage and tradition of the church and share that experience through their corporate activity in the world.

"My thesis," wrote Ellis Nelson in his book *Where Faith Begins*, "is that faith is communicated by a community of believers and that the meaning of faith is developed by its members out of their history, by their interaction with each other, and in relation to the events that take place in their lives." [2] I agree.

Frequently we have tended to behave as if Christian education were exclusively or primarily classroom instruction in the Bible or explanation of beliefs through sermons and lectures. Increasingly it will be necessary to place an emphasis upon the experiential aspects of all planned and unplanned learning which takes place in the faith community.

Take forgiveness, for example. The church is often the last (rather than the first) place a person in need of acceptance or "love for nothing" can expect to receive it freely. Yet without that experience, instruction in the nature of grace will be less than meaningful. The first concern of church education needs to be the life of the community where the experience of the Christian faith can be made real. Only then will the educational task of interpretation have significance.

Paul Tillich described the church's educational task as

introducing each new generation into the life and mission of the faith community. He explained that this happens through experience or participation in the community and through identification and interpretation of the experience. One without the other is a denial of the church's educational ministry.

The problems of church education therefore are not to be attributed to an inept church school. No matter what the inadequacies of church schools, church school teachers, or church school curriculum, the problems which prevent church education from reaching its goals are within the life of congregations and their failure to be communities of faith and mission, communities of action and reflection.

The church must once again take seriously that as an educating community it is called to be a witnessing and learning community of faith. Many of the implications of these remarks will be found in the following chapters. At this point we only want to make clear our contention that church education is not just one aspect of the church's life, but integral to its total life.

There are those who believe that the institutional church will die. I do not. Rather I concur with Krister Stendahl, who said, "It is unrealistic to believe that 'institutional religion' will fade away. There will of course be substantial changes in the structure of these institutions, but that does not make them less institutional." [3] But reform there must be. And I sense that here and there new life is appearing. The reform I speak of is radical reform— radical meaning fundamental, going to the roots or origin.

Because of its position in the world, the early church was truly an educating—learning and witnessing—faith community of committed—acting and reflecting—Christians. For too long Christianity has been a favored "official" religion in our society. The church has been secure and privileged; to be known as a Christian has been popular, to belong to a church, socially accepted. But as long as the church cannot be distinguished from the culture, and the life of its people cannot be distinguished from the lives of other people, church education will remain without an adequate foundation.

I sense, however, that something very important is occurring. The church may for the first time since the third century be free from the bondage of cultural acceptance and state support. Once again, the church finds itself on the fringes of society. These changing circumstances provide exciting new possibilities for the church to become a truly dynamic learning and witnessing faith community. The church is once again in radical reformation. That's good. Also painful, as birth pangs are.

Those of us who are committed to the faith community live between the times. That explains the reason for the tension in the church and the confusion about the shape of its life and educational ministry. Some want the church to be now what it can only be in the future; others want it to remain what it could only be in the past; thus the estrangement between the reformer and many parishioners increases. That gap needs to be closed. Together we can question and plan. We can experiment with many new models and begin the construction of a viable alternative for the church and its educational ministry.

This will require asking some new questions and being open to new answers. Church educators used to ask, "How can the church school build a new community of faith?" Today we had better ask, "How can a reformed church create a new model for church education?" The answer to that question is problematic but it is at least the right question. The hope of the future is with those local congregations who answer it creatively. At stake are tomorrow's children.

II. WHERE WE WERE

There is no need for us to repeat the errors of our fathers, or be ignorant of their wisdom. By exploring our history we can enlighten our judgments about the present and be liberated from the prison of our own experience. Historical knowledge can also sober those of us who sometimes think we know the certain solutions to our present educational problems; it can free those who believe we can return to a past that no longer exists.

History is written for self-understanding. Our purpose in reading men's memory of the past is to gain insight and direction for the future. The aim of studying current historical trends is not to learn what is likely to occur, but what we ought to make happen. The value of historical inquiry is in the consequent actions which result from a broadened perspective. In that sense, a look backward can be a look forward. The mirror of history frees us from always having to start from scratch, saves us from accepting easy dogmatisms which appear either new or sanctified by age, and it prevents us from romanticizing our past, which can immobilize us when we must meet the demands of the present. We study history to stretch our minds and force ourselves out of contemporary ruts. Planning an alternative future for church education obviously requires an understanding of our past.

Yet if we ask most Protestants to tell us about church education they will begin with tales of their own Sunday school experience. It is amazing how many of us are unaware of the Sunday school's brief and checkered history. Many of its defendants and critics do not realize the full significance of this two-hundred-year-old institution. That history still remains to be fully written. However the story of religious education in America begins somewhere else.

The dominant educational theory in early America was drawn from European-English Protestantism. Bringing Christianity to American soil was part and parcel of the colonization movement. At the beginning of this expansion almost every country had its established church. Religious homogeneity was considered to be essential to the stability of the social order and the strength of the state. Obviously there was little place for religious toleration. For those who were "different," America became a haven in which they could express their interpretation of life and the Christian faith. Yet naturally when they reached America, they transferred as much as possible of the state-church system which had persecuted them abroad. In their established homogeneous communities, education took place primarily through a process best described as induction.

Induction simply refers to the education of persons through their participation in family, church, and community. Induction preceded interpretation, but interpretation made induction complete. Interpretation took place primarily in the home. For many years the law of Massachusetts required that all families catechize their children and servants at least once a week. While the law was not always obeyed there was little question about the importance of the family for nurture and instruction. In the same manner the church and schools in a community became significant to a person's religious education. The school reinforced, through instruction, the nurture of home and church. Children in many of the town schools of New England learned their alphabet: A = "In Adam's fall, we sinned all," to Z = "Zacchaeus, he did climb a tree his Lord to see." Education was understood as the total life of a person in community and the interpretation of that experience in his home, church, and town school. Christian education was not so much a distinct form of education as an integral and natural part of daily life.

The difficulties of Christian education through induction increased as men and women of different religious persuasions moved into these once homogeneous communities. The American scene was changing.

With the establishment of the United States of America, the thirteen states, in recognition of their religious diversity, began to separate church and state by affirming freedom in religion. While the process of separation was not complete until 1833, a revolutionary event in both political and religious history had begun. Its full impact is just beginning to be felt in our own day.

In those states where immigration was substantial, the effects of this separation were significant. Life in such communities could no longer be counted upon to nurture children as Protestant Christians. The situation in the schools was somewhat different. Since most communities remained predominantly Protestant, the schools continued to be expressive of a Protestant ethos. (Parenthetically I might mention that this is one reason why Protestants have given such wholehearted support to the public schools and Roman Catholics have concluded that they needed parochial schools for the education of their children. It also helps us understand why the last vestige of Protestant religion is being removed from the public schools in our day of secular religious pluralistic communities. But that gets too far ahead of our story.)

Shortly after the Revolutionary War another movement began in England which would have a tremendous influence on American religious education. In 1780, a newspaperman by the name of Robert Raikes became concerned with delinquency and illiteracy in the cities of England. Convinced that London's problems would be solved if he could get the waifs off the slum streets and teach them to read, he established a school which met on Sunday (the one day these children were not forced to work in the factory). Taking a group of children from six to fourteen years of age into a private home, he attempted to teach them reading and writing. The Bible was the natural choice for a textbook. In the next thirty years half a million children were involved in these self-supporting lay organizations known as Sunday schools.

For the most part the Sunday school movement was opposed by many churchmen on two counts. First, it broke the fourth commandment concerning the Sabbath; second, the privileged classes, who for the most part made up the churches, did not believe that these children ought to be educated. Sure that these schools would only cause trouble, they described them as instruments of the devil.

But the idea of a Sunday school immediately found sympathetic ears across the ocean. Five years later the first such school was founded in America. You might call these schools the birth of our American "head start" program.

In Virginia two Sunday schools were established, one for poor whites and the other for black slaves. Both attempted to teach these children to read and write.

Shortly thereafter "head start" Sunday schools which taught children to read the Bible were established in Philadelphia, the new republic's largest city. The intent was the same: to aid "ignorant and lawless children."

A careful reading of the early history of the Sunday school can make one quite romantic about its contribution to education in America. An accurate evaluation of its importance for religious education may be beyond us, but we do owe these lay Sunday schools a debt of gratitude. For many children these were the only schools they knew. Only the privileged had the opportunity to attend those schools which later in the colonies were to become "public" or "common" schools.

The Sunday school movement spread rapidly throughout the country. Yet it was nearly a generation before these schools for the underprivileged, taught by lay volunteers, were appreciated or in some instances even tolerated by the church. It was only those denominations whose constituency came primarily from the lower social classes which were prepared to immediately accept the Sunday school.

Since the churches of the disenfranchised led the Western expansion, the Sunday school went with them, providing general as well as religious education for all the children of the frontier. Thus the Sunday school became the forerunner of the public school and the church in much of America.

However, as the public school system developed, the Sunday school assumed a more specialized function. The public school and the Sunday school became supportive institutions; together they provided the religious education of the young. The public school remained the primary agency for religious education (from a Protestant perspective). The Sunday school taught the tenets of particular Protestant denominations. The importance of the one-hour-a-week Sunday schools run by volunteers can be understood only on the basis of the widespread Protestant dependence upon the public school for the fundamental aspects of religious education.

With its goal of conversion, the Sunday school in America first emphasized memorizing the catechism, then shifted to Bible study—that is, to memorizing the Bible. Most denominations slowly adopted the Sunday school, using a common Bible-centered curriculum. The Sunday schools remained lay-dominated, largely for children, strongly evangelistic, and staffed by untrained but highly committed teachers.

The Sunday school in the minds of most American Protestants was equivalent to church education. We do not know what children thought about the Sunday school. Its success or failure can't adequately be measured. The glowing reports of its proponents and the scathing reactions of its critics provide only partial insight into its importance.

One caricature of these Sunday schools is found in *The Adventures of Tom Sawyer*. He told how Tom's Sunday school gave tickets as prizes for memorizing Bible verses. The aim was to earn enough to win a Bible. Tom wasn't too good at memorization but he was smart enough to trade chalk and other items he gained from his friends for tickets. One Sunday he went to Sunday school, listened to the superintendent's speech, delivered amidst fidgeting and the throwing of paper wads, and then went up to get his prize. The judge who was awarding the Bible made the mistake of asking him to name the first two disciples.

After much prompting he stammered, "David and Goliath."

During these early days of the Sunday school movement, children were seen as sinners who needed to be converted, i.e., saved from sin. The Sunday school hoped to convince them of their fallen state and their need for salvation.

In the middle of the nineteenth century, Horace Bushnell attempted to suggest a different goal for religious education. He attacked the Sunday school's emphasis on conversion. Bushnell held that children did not need to be converted from sin, but rather saved from falling into sin. The proper method of education was nurture. A child was "to grow up a Christian and never know himself as anything else." He was too radical; his position was vigorously opposed or worse, ignored. Traditionalism pervaded much of the Sunday school movement.

Many Sunday schools operated as separate institutions which made use of church buildings. Often those who controlled the Sunday school and taught in its classes did not participate in other aspects of the church life; those who attended an "opening exercise" in the Sunday school would not be found at the church's services of worship.

The Sunday school in many churches remained an adjunct institution, financially and organizationally independent. Its ethos tended to be oriented to the past. Yet on occasion in some churches, in various parts of the country, it was in the forefront of theological endeavors, with the church trailing behind.

The twentieth century marked some dramatic shifts in child psychology and education. John Dewey ushered in the progressive era. A new liberal theology evolved and the religious education movement was born. Although once criticized, Bushnell became a hero and some churchmen began to think seriously about education in a new key. An interfaith educational movement was envisioned as the means by which a new world could be built. Many church educators were optimistic about man. They pointed out that children were not sponges who absorbed religion, nor empty vessels to be filled with memory verses. Religion was to be part of the human experience; a child was to learn by doing. Thus there was a shift from the biblical content-centered curriculum produced by the American Sunday School Union to a child-centered, closely graded curriculum published ecumenically.

The first two decades of this century were times of experimentation. In 1905, a weekday school for Christian education was begun in the new industrial city of Gary, Indiana. An ecumenical city board of religious education was created to organize a city system of Christian religious schools on a released time basis.

Numerous other attempts were made to keep the church school abreast of public education. An increasing number of leaders were beginning to suggest that a new form of church education would have to be developed. Walter Athearn, a professor of religious education at Boston University, wrote:

> I am concerned with a fair division of the child's time among the various educational agencies of the community. . . . We need to build a system of church schools which will parallel our system of public schools and be equally efficient. . . . The church must have a share of the week's days for religious education.[1]

His proposal resulted in what was known as the Malden plan. In Malden, Massachusetts a community-wide program of weekday religious schools that shared a child's time with the public school during the school year was developed. That was in 1917. Some leaders in religious education would settle for nothing less than a first-rate system of weekday schools staffed by professionally trained teachers and supervised by a community board of religious education, made up of laymen representing different denominations.

Much of what we regard today as new models of religious education can be found in the literature of the 1920's. Unfortunately, many of their innovations remained limited to a few experiments. In general, Protestants were not interested in developing a new program of Christian education. Most believed that the public school and an hour a week on Sunday with volunteer teachers was fully satisfactory.

For the most part the religious education movement remained a professional movement. Its influence was felt primarily in the seminaries and national boards of mainline Protestant denominations rather than in congregations. An experiment was tried here and there and some ideas infiltrated the church, but to all intents and purposes church education continued as a lay dominated Sunday school. Denominational educational boards produced numerous paper resources for educational innovation. The churches did not overwhelmingly accept them and even where they did, teachers' behavior was rarely affected by them. This is a lesson we ought not to forget.

It is important to note, however, that while enormous change did not take place in church education, significant improvement in church schooling did. As long as the church school and the public school were understood as parallel institutions yoked together in a common concern, Christian education had a focus and a force.

With the dawn of the twentieth century hope for the results which could emerge from these joint educational endeavors blossomed. The thirties, however, saw some major shifts in American religious life. The Religious Education movement appeared to be dying. Men were not so optimistic about progress, man, or the possibility that education could save the world. A new era in theology appeared with Barth, Brunner, Niebuhr and Tillich. The church began to look at itself and be interested in renewal. Two new concerns appeared: Christian education with a distinct theological content, and the church school as a unique place where local congregations carried out a particular kind of education. Denominations concluded that they had to create their own curriculums, i.e., courses to be run for their own church schools.

Some chose to emphasize the content of theology; others, a teaching method that was theologically sound. For the first, instruction in Bible, theology, and church history became central to what children and youth (and adults) were taught in the church school. For the latter nurture through interpersonal relationships became the experiential base for learning. Still others tried to steer a middle course. All of them took church education seriously as they attempted to build their churches into learning and witnessing faith communities. Professional educators began to be trained to equip the church for its task.

The process of such reform movements continues. Denominations plan and publish new curriculum resources for church schools, establish teacher training institutes and procedures, and other such means for improving church education. New church school plants are constructed, new media such as television and film are put to use in a few multi-media learning centers. Once again, churches experiment with ecumenical weekday schools and a variety of improved methods of teaching, including ungraded classes, team teaching and the like. Concern for church schooling and improved educational resources mounts. Traditional models continue to get better. They should, but we also need to develop some new strategies.

Robert Lynn made clear the reason in his *Protestant Strategies in Education.*[2] He suggests that Protestant education faces a crisis because it is not aware of the major shifts that have taken place in our society. Those shifts have destroyed the parallelism upon which Protestant church education has been based. Lynn referred to the Supreme Court's rulings on prayer and Bible reading, "The court was completing a process begun years ago in many communities and states: the gradual elimination of the practices of the Protestant-dominated common school of the last century." And he concluded:

> Protestants . . . cannot go . . . back to the nineteenth century. . . . Public schools can no longer embody just the Protestant ethos if they are to be genuinely public institutions. In a society such as ours, it is truly unrealistic and irresponsible to depend upon the public school as a silent partner in the task of Christian education.[3]

While acknowledging the end of an era of parallelism we need to face the new challenge which is before us.

The ethos of the American culture is becoming more pluralistic. As high mobility moves people from place to place, communities incorporate a whirling variety of life styles and value systems. With the decline of the cultures of small town enclaves, fewer communities provide a particular understanding of life or behavior. The universal availability of mass media only compounds the problem.

We cannot expect the public schools in such pluralistic communities to teach any single value system or attempt to instruct or nurture children in a particular life style. With the increasing breakdown of the extended family, we can no longer expect that the generations together will pass on a sense of tradition.

Nor can we anticipate that the church or the church's school as we have known them can meet our educational needs. We only have to look at the new generation to realize that our residual confidence in the present patterns of church life and education is untenable. To talk about what the church school did for us is to fail to understand the dramatic changes that have taken place in American culture. We cannot assume that modernizing or improving church education according to past models will save us. But a new possibility for an alternative future awaits us.

I am not anxious to defame the church school as some critics have done, but only to reveal its inadequacy for our present time. If we recognize the church school's historical validity and growth, we do not need either to defend or condemn it. What we need to do is explore beyond it—to seek an alternative for the future.

Most periods in history are dominated either by trends or opportunities. We know that change and innovation are difficult during a trend period. But other periods provide occasions when change and innovation can more easily occur. I suggest that today we are provided with a period of opportunity for change and innovation. Another way to put it—our times are open to the new. Reform is possible. Innovation to meet changing times and new demands is within our grasp. Ours is a period ripe for an alternative future.

III. NOT WHAT BUT HOW

What a person learns is a concern of educators. It ought to be. But what is it that Christian educators hope persons will learn? Do the "how" and "where" we learn help to determine "what" we learn? Does the context in which we teach shape our content? Is the way we learn important for communicating what we intend a person to know? In other words, should we emphasize the educational process?

Conversations with church school teachers reveal that they understand education as primarily imparting information. They believe that children, youth and sometimes adults need to be told what the Bible says, what occurred in the history of the church, what Christians believe, and what right or wrong behavior is. Parents are saying we need to reemphasize such information in church education.

Certainly such knowledge is of some importance. The Bible is an essential document for the Christian church. But what is it about the Bible that makes it valuable? Is it the thoughts and stories within its pages? Or is it how those whose heritage we share spied God's activity in the world; how they decided his will for them? And say we acknowledge the second, do we want to teach others what men in the past discovered, or do we want to enable persons to make discoveries of their own?

Without question, the beliefs, doctrines, and ethical guidelines which the church has expounded through the ages are significant. But is learning about them the only crucial matter, or is it rather learning the thinking process which led to framing them? If we affirm the second, how can people today learn that process of theological and ethical reflection?

When we say we want to communicate the Christian faith, what do we mean? Do we want to teach information about the Christian faith, or do we want to introduce persons to the Christian faith? If the second is our goal, how do we accomplish it? What is faith?

Most often faith is misunderstood as a set of specific beliefs expressed through special words. People explain, "To be a Christian is to believe that . . . ." But Christian faith does not involve believing that particular statements are true. It certainly does not mean intellectual assent to a creed or certain words found in a translation of the Bible.

All beliefs are relative. They are the important but historically conditioned attempts of men to express their faith; they are not its equivalent. Remember that there was a time when men believed that the world was created in six days. But belief in one age may stand in the way of understanding in another. That is why today we can say that it is not essential for a Christian to believe in a literal virgin birth. Instead we must seek to understand the meaning behind such words when used by third-century Christians to express their faith so that we can do the same in our day.

Every religion possesses a set of historical doctrines and practices, beliefs and customs. We don't always learn a great deal about a man's religion by studying such things. Christianity cannot be understood until we understand Christians. We do not really understand Christians by asking them to tell us to state in words what they believe. Moreover, faith must be expressed afresh by men in every age. Yet faith is never identical with these stated beliefs; it is a reality beyond them.

Nor is faith to be understood primarily as particular feelings. It is not to be equated with the subjective emotional response that comes with seeing a sunset or standing hand in hand at a peace demonstration. Many adults who personally have difficulty believing the host of doctrines they think Christian faith demands turn to subjective emotions. It is easier to live with that glow which results from "mountain top" experiences. No understanding is required of emotions nor is any particular behavior. With his "religion" put safely in the corner of subjective feelings one can live in most any way he wishes. Think of all the people who have been given the impression that faith can be identified with singing hymns in a candlelight chapel grove. Or recall the early days of the civil rights movement when many of us Northern liberals identified faith with that good feeling which accompanied our marches in the South while unaware of our own racism. But faith cannot be understood only as feelings, even good feelings.

Neither is faith particular actions. It is not to be identified with a "religious" act such as going to church or praying. Think of all the people who have been told in church school that those who affirm the Christian faith say their prayers every night, read their Bibles regularly and attend church every Sunday.

Faith certainly is not standing at attention when the American flag goes by or joining the army because your country calls you to fight what you believe to be an unjust war. It cannot be identified with being polite to one's elders, or obeying laws, or even giving Thanksgiving baskets to the poor. Nor can faith be identified with resisting the draft or boycotting grapes. Faith surely demands action, but it cannot be specifically identified with particular prescribed actions, "religious" or otherwise.

In the history of the church all kinds of errors have been perpetuated and taught by those who called themselves Christians. Once men believed that as Christians they were saved and other men damned, that they knew God and were right while other men did not and were totally wrong. Once those who called themselves Christians felt that white men were superior to black men and that people were poor because God willed it, or because they didn't work hard enough. Once churchmen acted as if holy wars and crusades against those they classified as infidels were the will of God and therefore just. To identify such beliefs, attitudes or actions with the Christian faith would be a catastrophe.

Surely faith in every age must be expressed in terms of beliefs, must be felt in the depths of men's hearts, and actualized through their behavior. Faith is all of this but much more. Faith transcends all its historically conditioned representations. It is deeper than all its expressions.

To understand a man's faith we must get inside the way he sees the world. Faith is best comprehended as a person's frame of reference, as the eyes through which he looks at life and views his own life. All our beliefs, feelings, and actions issue from our faith. Our faith in turn issues from our life experiences. Therefore, in order for a person to be introduced to the Christian faith, education is going to have to be understood as more than classroom instruction, more than imparting information about what the Bible says, what occurred in the history of the church, what Christians believe, or what right and wrong behavior is.

If we want a person to be able to accept or reject the Christian faith, we have to turn our attention and emphasis from teaching about Christianity to offering within the church experiences which demonstrate our faith. Education needs to become the conscious process by which we share our way of looking at life and our values, induct persons into our lifestyle, and help them discover their own self-identity.

Faith results from experiences, associations, and relationships which we can think about, but which cannot be produced by thinking. The community of faith is the place where a particular way of looking at life is expressed, fostered, and given meaning. Faith is communicated by participation in the total life of such a community. Our faith issues from our experiences; its meaning, however, is acquired by a process of action and reflection. We discover what the Christian frame of reference implies by acting and reflecting with those who share that faith. For that reason, church education also needs to change its focus from learning about Christian doctrine and tradition to learning how a Christian acts and thinks.

This implies a change of emphasis from "content" (what we teach) to "process" (how and where we teach). It used to make sense to ask someone, "What do you teach?" That question has become somewhat meaningless. Of more significance are questions like: Where do you think? How do you think?

Not What but How 29

Those questions are much more difficult to answer, but their importance is crucial. Consider: *What* we think is determined far more than we realize by *where* we think and *why* we think. Where we think is what we think. How we think is what we think. Why we think is what we think. The where, how, and why questions are the crucial questions for church education.

We sometimes forget that the way we teach is what we teach. When our aim is the communication of information and ideas, we can teach through assigned readings and classroom lectures, supplemented by questions for discussion. But when our objective is a process of reflection on important social issues and private concerns, then such methods may not only be inadequate but actually destructive.

To learn the process of thinking in the light of a Christian frame of reference implies opportunities for practice. Involvement and participation are essential. What might they look like?

An upper management program at a university business school may be a helpful case study. In the past, this business school offered corporation executives a course in business ethics, taught by a theologian. Each day he came from one end of the campus to the other, armed with a prepared lecture for his note-taking students. After answering a few questions, he would return to his library office to prepare his next lecture. For both students and teacher, the course began and ended in that classroom. The teacher obviously expected his students to apply their newly acquired knowledge to their work. It never seemed to happen.

One day, the Dean concluded that something was wrong with the way this subject was taught and he made some changes. No more would theologians be brought in to lecture; no more would businessmen be offered a course in business ethics. Instead, a few theologians would be invited to fully participate in the program. Theologians would live, eat and play together and discuss actual case studies with the businessmen. They would join in their daily attempts to find solutions to their most pressing corporation problems. The aim: to learn to think theologically about issues. They would help each other learn, not by telling each other what to believe or do, but by striving together to solve mutual problems.

The first few meetings were a struggle. Each group was overly conscious of the other. The theologians struggled to be "good businessmen"; the businessmen to be "good theologians." Then something happened. They were discussing a shoe manufacturing company case.

Let me over-simplify that discussion. There were two executives: a personnel manager and a vice president. It appeared that the personnel manager was very much concerned about the company's employees. One couldn't help liking him. He treated every employee in what some would call a "Christian" way. The vice president, on the other hand, was difficult to like. He seemed to be the "typical" cut-throat businessman. A policy conflict emerged between them which could not be resolved. One of them had to be released.

In discussing the case, the business executives tried very hard to be ethical. They had almost convinced each other that the vice president had to go when one of the theologians said, "I don't know a great deal about running a business, but it seems to me that the shoe manufacturing business is highly competitive and there is a very slim profit margin. Shoe corporations easily go bankrupt. This community has no other industry. This company is the major source of employment. If the company gets into economic difficulty and has to close or move, the community will be brought to the brink of disaster. Only if the company makes a profit and stays in business will these people have food, clothes, and a roof over their heads. I don't like the vice president any better than you do. But under these peculiar circumstances, I think he is the one showing the most love for these people by his apparent ruthlessness. Perhaps in this situation, the personnel manager should be released." And then the discussions became exciting and relevant.

Such an engagement with a real life issue provided the necessary context to learn the process of theological reflection and moral action. That was only a limited beginning. But it was at least a relevant start. Church education needs to enable persons to integrate Christian doctrine with issues, to make enlightened responses in faith to the demands of a rapid and radically changing world, to become self-conscious Christians.

The task of church education is to help us make sense out of life and the issues that confront us, to make clear what options we have and to enable us to decide what we should be and do. What is usually called church education often turns out only to be long tirades on yesterday's pieties and the puzzles of antiquarian thought rather than a confrontation with the issues which face the man of faith in a changing world.

Our educational task is not prescribing right actions for people but helping them learn how to answer the question: What are we as believers in Christ and members of his church to do? Church education is to help us learn to be responsible decision makers, men and women who have the capacity and will to act on issues such as open housing, war, foreign aid, socialized medicine, or a guaranteed annual income.

Church education therefore needs to focus its attention on occasions where persons can experience the Christian faith and learn how to think and act on issues in the light of that faith. It is my contention that while this might occur in classrooms, it will be more likely to occur through participation in the life of a congregation and in groups gathered somewhere in the community to deal with those specific social issues that demand action.

IV. ACT IT OUT!

One night I sat on the bare floor of a cold room in the slums of a small city. A single sixty-watt bulb hung from the cracked ceiling, dimly lighting the room. With me were a small group of college students. They thought of themselves as a church. A year before they had committed themselves to life in community. While completing their studies at the university in such diverse fields as education, sociology, English literature, religion and history, they had come together to prepare themselves for what they called "Christian citizenship." They felt that neither the churches they knew nor the university, were adequately equipping them to act as responsible members of society.

Their quest was for a Christian education. That is, education which would prepare them to live meaningful and purposeful lives in our world, where welfare and poverty remain formidable problems, where human rights and justice are not yet a reality for all men, and peace is still only a Christmas hope. As one girl put it, "We need to be equipped with the human skills and values which can meet the needs of our world." Others made clear that they wanted to be able to act, to feel, to think, to value, goals they could not reach so long as education was separated from life. They acknowledged that it was foolish to assume they could become feeling, behaving beings through study in classrooms which by their very nature were estranged from the events of daily life. No one, they believed, could really understand the political process by reading about it or listening to lectures or even participating in discussions. More could be learned from working for a political cause.

A young priest who taught at the university agreed with them. So much so that he had joined them. "Churches think of religious education as discussing problems in church," he said. "We do not relate thought to action. We study issues to death. We affirm the need for action but we rarely get around to acting. How did we ever forget that behavior—action—is what education is all about? We only learn how to act by acting. That's what we're here for. This is our laboratory for Christian education and we are trying to develop a new model for what we call action-study."

And so they were. That evening the community had their attention. During the past year a number of their poor neighbors had died while being transferred, before treatment, from the nearby private hospital to the city hospital on the other side of the city. They knew two of them. One had been a young boy they were tutoring, the other a mother whose children they had cared for so she could go to work. The issue was clear. How could they change the system that had created this problem? Together they would have to work out an action strategy. Yes, and they would act. Later they would reflect. In the process they would learn what it means to behave as a Christian.

All too infrequently does participation in the Christian education program of local congregations prepare persons to behave as responsible citizens. Why not? Because we have thought of church education as study rather than action. Because we haven't really taken seriously what it means for education to enable a person to become human. If man is essentially an actor, church education should help him to understand himself as such.

Each of our lives has been influenced by other men's actions. In spite of the fact that some like to affirm that they are self-made men, there is little evidence to support that claim. In our reflective moments we honestly admit that we are largely a result of our past.

Where I was born, when, to what parents, the town in which I was raised, the schools I attended, the people I knew, the churches I served, the books I read, the places I visited, the woman I married have all influenced me more than I might like to admit. To a major extent, I am a result of my experiences. You are the result of yours.

Norbert Wiener in his autobiography comments about the importance of his ancestry:

> The Jewish family structure is somewhat closer than the average European family structure, and much closer than that of America. Whether the Jews have had to meet a religious prejudice or a racial prejudice or simply minority prejudice, they have had to meet hostile prejudice, and even though this may be disappearing in many cases, the Jews are well aware of it, and it has modified their psychology and their attitude toward life. When I speak of Jews and myself as a Jew, I am merely stating the historical fact that I am descended from those belonging to a community which has a certain tradition and body of attitudes, both religious and secular, and that I should be aware of the ways in which I myself and those around me

have been conditioned by the very existence of this body of attitudes.[1]

We cannot understand who we are or who other men are without realizing the degree to which we are all products of other men's actions. But we are more, much more.

Surely, when we look at our lives, we realize how much we are both positively and negatively influenced by forces outside our control. Yet in our sober moments we also know that we make ourselves. We each make decisions. We act, and our actions shape our lives.

When we think about it, there is rarely a week that goes by in which we don't determine to some extent our futures. To be sure, unlimited options are not always open to us. But think of what our lives might be like today if we did (or did not): go to college, marry, have children, accept our present job, live where we do, and so forth. In each of our decisions, we exercise our freedom from outside forces and determine the future course of our lives.

You and I decide daily. In those decisions is our potential freedom. The black man in the ghetto who is cut off from life becomes a free man on the day he decides to be proud and black, the day he decides to stand up before a white racist society and demand reparation for the evil a white society has heaped on his head.

The over-burdened, unstimulated housewife whose abilities and talents remain untapped because she lives in a society dominated by men and their values becomes a free person the day she decides to rise up and secure the position she is capable of by establishing a new way to raise her children and take care of her home so she can also do what she wants to do.

If we are to be free we must act, remembering that no decision is one hundred percent private. We need to learn to ask those questions which can help us anticipate how our decisions will affect others, and thus learn how to be part of our society's decision making processes.

When we always let someone else decide for us, we are less than fully human. At the trial of Adolf Eichmann the world saw a man who looked much like many of us, a man who simply by doing what he was told (i.e. by efficiently keeping the trains rolling) took the lives of hundreds of innocent men, women and children.

The accused were not alone at the Nuremberg War Crimes Trials; a whole nation was before the judges' seat. The court tried only a few men. They didn't look like criminals; they had been teachers, lawyers, bank clerks, opera singers. One was a minister. The refrain of their defense rang: "You must understand I only followed orders." While I do not believe that justifies their actions, neither do I believe that they alone are to be condemned. The parents, schools, churches and communities that nurtured them and taught them to simply follow orders share a responsibility for their actions.

At those trials, we taught the world, and especially our youth, that each of us is responsible for what he does no matter who makes the decision to do it. We also taught them that we are responsible for decisions and actions carried out by the institutions of which we are a part. Is it any wonder that we witness a new moral sensibility on our college campuses? Many of our students have taken seriously what we taught them about man. That is one reason so many of our most sensitive and brightest students have taken to the streets in order to influence the decisions of their country on the war in Vietnam, the ROTC, college military research, university expansion, and black demands for equality and justice. A critique can easily be written on them for they are not always willing to pay the personal price for their actions. And often their moral purity is self-deceptive. But the important gain is their awareness of responsibility for decision making on behalf of society.

The heroes of this new generation are likely to be men like Dietrich Bonhoeffer who said, "We are called to be a man and to be a man for others." Bonhoeffer could have stayed safely in an American seminary, but he decided he must return to Hitler's Germany. He explained to Reinhold Niebuhr why he was leaving with these words:

> I shall have no right to participate in the reconstruction of Christian life in Germany after the war if I do not share the trials of this time with my people. . . . Christians in Germany will face the terrible alternative of either willing the defeat of their nation in order that Christian civilization may survive, or willing the victory of their nation and thereby destroying our civilization. I know which of these alternatives I must choose.[2]

Bonhoeffer made his choice and died a martyr's death. He was a product of his past, but he also determined his life and the lives of all of us by his actions.

Enabling persons to make responsible decisions—to act, to reflect upon their actions—is the aim of church education. Only such learning will make it possible for a person to become human, for man is essentially an actor.

Winfred Cantwell Smith of the Harvard Center for World Religion suggests in a lecture entitled "Christian—Noun or Adjective?" that if someone asks "Are you a Christian?" one can answer glibly, "yes," or "no." If, however, someone asks you if you are Christian, the situation changes radically. You cannot give a yes or no answer to that question. In fact he suggests that the question really ought to be "How Christian are you?" He writes:

Our section of town might become Christian in certainly a deeper, certainly a different sense if we persons who inhabit it could rise to being Christian, and not merely Christians . . .

It would require a good deal of effort, and not a little grace, to make a quarter (of our town) *Christian* . . . whereas with no effort at all and perhaps even no grace at all, it can be labeled Christian.[3]

To judge whether a person is Christian we look at his total behavior in a moment of time. Educating a person to be a Christian involves giving him facts and information; it implies telling him a lot about Christianity. Educating a person to be Christian is quite different. It is inviting him to participate actively in the life of a community of those who "act Christian."

A person cannot learn to be a physician without the experience of treating patients. No one can learn to be a painter without painting, a mother without having children, a Christian without being Christian. In other words we do not learn what it is to be Christian by studying about Christianity.

We are hung up on classroom study in church education. Just visit an average church and ask someone to show you its educational program. Will you be taken to a worship service, a social action committee working for the election of one of their members to the school board, a group planning to participate in a march on the capital, or to visit a number of families in the parish? No! In most cases, you will be taken to Sunday morning classes where most likely an adult will be telling children and youth about Christian beliefs and customs.

You may not believe the following example, but it is true. Not long ago I was passing through a church school and I looked in on a junior high school class. There in front of a group of what apparently had been some noisy boys was a male teacher standing at a lectern. His face was red and he was pounding on the lectern and shouting at the top of his lungs, "Shut up or I'll toss you out of the room! I'll tell your parents to keep you at home. In fact if you don't behave I'm going to get the minister in here to talk to you. Now shut up! Otherwise how am I going to teach you about the unconditional love of God?" Amazing but true. Word for word. I'll never forget it. For too long we have assumed that the unthinking transmission of Christian history, behavior and ethics by a teacher in a classroom will enable persons to gain a knowledge of the Christian faith.

Most of us have connected study solely with thinking in a classroom with a teacher. A school is people who come together to think. Taking the next step of relating our thought to action, while important, is not considered the business of the schools. Is it any wonder that many middle-aged college graduates find it so easy to gather in groups to think and talk about problems and yet find it so difficult to take action? For years we have been conditioned to equate education with schooling and schooling with acquiring information and talking about problems. Of course, we affirm the need for action but taking action has always turned out to be something we did after we had completed our study of an issue. Study was supposed to lead to action but we know that in practice it often became an escape from involvement, action or even decision making. We seemed to believe that new thoughts would inevitably result in new actions. Instead we are discovering that we are much more likely "to act our way into a new way of thinking rather than think our way into a new way of acting."

We learn by doing. There is nothing new about that. The place to teach about a Christian understanding of citizenship is within a group of Christians who are both acting and reflecting on the issues which they face as citizens.

Neither the extreme of isolated reading and talking about social problems in a classroom of like-minded people, nor the extreme of mindless activism according to the current conventional wisdom provides an adequate model for Christian education.

As Dewey affirmed, we learn best through active participation in an acting-reflecting group. In the church we need groups involved in learning by doing, together with serious reflection, so that as Christians we can discover what we ought to do. We need opportunities to act so we may test our hunches and be responsible for our conclusions.

If we want new thoughts we need new experiences. If we want to grow in our understanding we need to be confronted by those who disagree with us. If we want to learn we need to act. But if we want to act as Christians we need to reflect on our actions within a Christian community.

Charles Lemert in Needham, Massachusetts, tells of a group of women gathered for six weeks of study on Christian ethics and world problems. It soon became apparent that a seminar on world problems was an absurd use of educational time. Instead, the group met with the director of the Commission on Housing for the United Church in Boston, who quickly put this small group of inexperienced, suburban women to work observing meetings of the Boston Housing Authority. They were greeted with instant hostility by the Authority, which was hypersensitive to outsiders meddling in official city business. The ladies, inexperienced in dealing with such situations, backed off. Suddenly, some of their schedules became busy and they weren't sure they could make it. One member was concerned over possible trouble for her husband's business. Basically, however, the problem was lack of experience. With gentle persuasion and support, the group finally kept its commitment to action.

In the end, their work produced very important results —their observations and research contributed to the publication of a study of the Boston Housing Authority which played a major role in increasing Boston's awareness of its housing problem and in producing progressive changes in the Authority itself.

For the women, the educational results were even more remarkable. They learned more about the urban world than any book could teach. By practical experience, they learned the skills of political research and confrontation. They no longer met the challenges of their less adventuresome suburban friends with platitudes, for they found that they were forced to develop a moral and theological rationale for their actions. At that point, theological and biblical material took on new meaning.

One member of the group became so skilled at political analysis and group leadership that she was elected the first full-time executive director of the newly formed Civil Rights Office in her community—a position of responsibility which would have been totally unthinkable for her just two years before. Virtually every member of the group has discovered a new sense of responsibility to her church and community. All are involved now in similar projects in their home town, bringing their newly acquired skills to bear on what, for them, is their primary responsibility: their own suburban community.

This is not merely a new form of "doing good" by tutoring "those poor kids" or throwing a party in a settlement house. Rather, it is effective participation in programs to confront, change and to reorganize those structures which prevent a unified society. Yet neither is it mindless activism. Rather, education becomes a process of reflective experience by participation in "the action" of Christian decision making.

Consider these thoughts: The martyr Dietrich Bonhoeffer wrote, "We shall never know what we do not do." The Spanish philosopher Unamuno wrote, "To be engaged in order to know." John Calvin, the Reformer, wrote, "True knowledge of God is born out of obedience." The author of *Christian Nurture*, Horace Bushnell, wrote, "No truth is really taught by words or interpreted by intellectual methods; truth must be lived into meaning before it can be fully known." And the theologian Karl Barth wrote, "Only the doer of the word is its real hearer."

In the Hebrew language "knowing" is an act of the will rather than the mind. "Knowing" is a submission in obedience to what is known. You do what you know. The interesting thing about the Hebrew concept of knowing is that it completely revolutionizes education. The Hebrews never assumed that "first they learn it and then they do it."

So it is in the Christian life—its beginning and end is action. We begin by participating in an acting faith community. No one can sit like a vegetable and study about Christianity and hope to understand it and thus be able to act Christian. We need to join others who are acting as Christians.

Too often we make the fundamental error of seeing education as preparation. Education as preparation for life becomes the postponement of life and in many cases even the crippling of life. We cannot make children and youth ready for participation in the faith community by isolat-

ing them in classes. Without full and meaningful participation in the total activity of the church, education becomes a parenthesis from life.

We cannot prepare persons for life without letting
them become involved. It is reflection on action that leads
to learning and growth. Together children, youth and
adults must have an opportunity to experience the
activity of the people of God and become involved in the
reflective action of the community of faith. Only then can
we call the church an educating community.

V. THE RIGHT START

There is a worn-out controversy which still rages in many churches. For some it is deadly serious. It is not an easy conflict to mediate, for neither side seems able to understand the other. Unfortunately, they have been caricatured as the "Bible-People" vs. the "Child-People." In the parish I discovered that the "Bible-People" thought me the enemy. The "Child-People" appeared overjoyed at being able to claim their minister as an ally. But I never really understood the apparently obvious disagreement.

Bearing my own confusion in mind, let me try to sort out the problem. Those unfairly caricatured as the "Bible-People" always asked the same question, "Why don't you teach the Bible?" The reply, "I do!" never satisfied them. They recalled their own early childhood experiences in a Sunday school where they learned to recite the books of the Bible, were drilled in memory verses, told Bible stories, and were lectured on what the Bible said about being a Christian. Apparently their Sunday school experiences had been considered favorable and information about the Bible acquired in those schools seemed meaningful and relevant. They desired the same for their children.

Most of those on the other side of the controversy could recall similar childhood experiences. Only they remembered them as negative and irrelevant. As a result, they wanted something else for their children. Religion, they affirmed, was part of everyday life; Christianity, they concluded, is a concern for persons. From telling Bible stories and memorizing verses they turned to the child's interests which resulted in what the "Bible-centered" people caricatured as "fun and games in the church."

Both sides were truly concerned for children, both interested in teaching the Bible. One group, in their emphasis on how children learn, sometimes forgot to ask what they intended to have them learn. The others, in their emphasis on what they wanted them to learn, forgot to ask the question of how people learn. In one sense both were right, although in another, both were wrong.

Most professional church educators resolved the problem more than a decade ago. Yet the misunderstanding and disagreement still continues among many laymen. Let me suggest a way out of the confusion. When we talk about church education, we are concerned about where to begin. Do we begin with persons, the Scriptures or . . . ? The battle to get lay church educators to take persons seriously has been long and hard. It is not over. Just talk to some preschool teachers and you discover how far we have to go. Yet many are aware of how children learn.

I remember a true story of a preschool class. One Sunday a harried teacher arrived knowing that her co-teacher was ill at home. As always seems to be true at such times more than the usual number of three-year-olds had arrived. Amidst the confusion the teacher noticed that Billy didn't look very well. His nose was running, his eyes watering. She wanted to find his mother before her whole class was contaminated. Just as she poked her head into the hall, another child screamed that Michael had dumped all the fish food into the fish bowl. While returning to rescue the fish, she overheard Jane quietly telling a friend: "My mommy went away last night and I cried." The teacher stopped short and listened. "The lady staying with me said if I didn't stop my mommy wouldn't come back."

Without another thought about her classroom crises, she put her arm around Jane and said: "Did you tell your mommy what the baby sitter said? I think she would like to know. Because mommies do come back, even if you cry. And I bet when your mommie comes home she tiptoes into your room to kiss you goodnight." Other children began to talk about times their mommies had gone away and come back. They sat on the floor and talked about it. Then before the teacher knew it, the mothers were arriving to pick up their children. Class was over. She hadn't read from the Bible, told the story that went with it, said the prayer, or done anything else she had planned. But it's possible that more Christian education occurred on *that* morning than on other mornings when more traditional things had been done.

People learn through experience. And besides, people are more important than subject matter. To permit *what* you teach to gain precedence over *whom* you teach is a grave error. Of course, teachers ought to affirm the centrality of people.

However, if we use individual persons as our only starting point for church education we may commit a serious error. One of the most critical problems we face today is individualism. We have grown up in a culture which proclaims individual freedom of life and expression as its highest good. The American church has blessed individualism. In an age confronted by overwhelming social problems we attempt to change individuals. In a nation whose social structures are racist we still attempt to deal with individual prejudice. In churches where people have lost their identity as well as contact with others, we have raised "sensitivity groups" to salvation heights. There is nothing wrong with attempts at changing individual thoughts, attitudes, or behavior, nor with opportunities for self-awareness and personal relationships. Yet I see little evidence that such changes in individuals have much effect on social issues or even on equipping individuals to deal with social problems. Needless to say, it is our inability to deal creatively with these social issues which may destroy us.

In American Protestant church education our emphasis on individualism and personal needs has proven inadequate. By starting with individual needs we have perpetuated a study of the Bible which searches for inspirational, devotional, and moral enlightenment for personal living, and little more. G. Ernest Wright, the biblical scholar and archeologist, has characterized what we tried to do by saying: "So convinced have we been that the true nature of religion consists in a dialogue between God and individual man that we have been quite willing to force the Bible to say what we want it to say." [1]

That describes the problem with person-centeredness. Another possibility is to begin with the biblical message itself. I can remember courses in which we studied the scriptures objectively attempting to understand the message within them. Do not underestimate the importance of such studies. For one thing I discovered that Jesus was not as concerned with saving individual persons as clearing the way for a new community of men. Even in the Sermon on the Mount he focused his attention on the nature of the kingdom (the new society) rather than upon individual behavior. To my surprise I learned that the Bible rather than giving primary attention to individuals is focused on two communities—Israel and the church. The message of the Bible is not so much concerned with individual living in the world, as the formation of these new communities and their social role in history. In the scriptures man is only a man when he is delivered from his big "I" and becomes a part of a new community in society. The Bible is not so much interested in his personal relationship to God or to other individuals, as in the people of God and the problems of society. But I don't need to rehearse the problems connected with the isolated study of the Bible, even when it is studied in an enlightened manner.

Another alternative exists. There is a way to maintain the importance of concern for people and the Bible while avoiding the traps of emphasizing one or the other. We can shift our emphasis to issues, that is, center our concern on social problems, using them as our starting point for church education. Then both individual needs and the message of the scriptures might be taken seriously.

I recall once walking through the halls of a hospital on my pastoral rounds. A doctor came out of a patient's room. He commented, "John, my oath as a physician to save life just doesn't make much sense any more. The woman in that room is 70 years old, her husband is dead, her family without much money. She is critically ill but because of modern science I can keep her alive in that vegetable state almost indefinitely. I'm faced with a new issue: Should I do so?" Before I could respond, he rushed off to an emergency.

A week later we began to meet regularly for lunch in the doctors' dining room of that hospital. A number of other doctors joined us. Each week one of them presented an issue for group discussion. We struggled to minister to each other's needs as we attempted to relate our biblical tradition to the issues confronting us.

Or take another case. A group of high school youth met in a local hangout for cokes and hamburgers to discuss the issues which bothered them. The group expanded to include some teachers and the questions they discussed had to do with education and schools. Other issue-centered groups emerged. One was concerned with the war in Vietnam, another with racism in a rural community, still another with welfare programs and the guaranteed annual income. By forming issue-centered educational opportunities we avoid the old hang-ups without ignoring the importance of either the Bible or people.

Individualism is one of the greatest evils Protestant churches must conquer. But individualistic biblicism runs a close second. The issues related to our world's social problems are crying to be addressed. Our times demand that we shift the emphasis of our programs in church education to those issues. Our day insists that we enable persons to deal with social issues such as racism, poverty, and war as they manifest themselves in our communities. In the past church education has not adequately attended to such concerns.

But a more impelling reason than past neglect is the Christian understanding of God and history.

To the question, Where is history going? comes the answer, The world is becoming the kingdom of God. God's reign over history is in the process of being realized. The fulfillment of God's purposes for men and mankind has begun. Turn around and accept the good news.

That is the core of Jesus' message; the message for which he was willing to leave his family, his job, his home, his security and for which he gave his life. Jesus did not contribute a set of improved prescriptions for right and wrong behavior, a better way of feeling about yourself and others, or a new and loftier set of beliefs about God. He summoned men to live each day with a different frame of reference—God's rule in history.

The Christian faith affirms that God is acting in the events of history. Man comes to know God as he acts to make our world over into a more human place. We become human as we begin to participate in God's history saving and kingdom building. Church education provides the context for us to grow in this faith by helping us to sense the activity of God and make those decisions which enable us to become God's ally in his community making.

Where, then, do we begin church education? Not with isolated individuals or an isolated document, the Bible, but with the issues and events of life and history, the arena where God acts and is known.

VI. DOWN WITH SCHOOL!

There is a strong tendency among many adults to look back on their Sunday school days with dewy-eyed nostalgia. Few contemporary youngsters share such feelings. Instead of fondness, they express discontent and discomfort. Witness the overwhelming dropout rate among students who have reached the age of independence. Better yet, cast an observant eye on the behavior of the psychologically dropped-out, found abundantly in every church school classroom. Learning ought to be an exciting activity and religious education engaging and meaningful. Nevertheless students tell me it is boring and dull. Testing those who attend and those who do not attend church schools reveals only minor differences in knowledge of the Christian faith; behavior differs not at all.

Once we thought our problem was caused by an irrelevant curriculum. So we responded with attempts to match student interest with class lessons. While certainly an improvement, these attempts did not seem to solve our problem. Our conclusion: teaching must be improved. We began to explore new ways to teach. Once they were refined, we proudly attempted to pass on our latest teaching methodology to every church school teacher. Better. But still not the solution.

As long as we maintain what I call a "teaching ghetto" mentality our problem will never be resolved. Such a mindset focuses on schooling or classroom instruction as the primary place of church education. That, I suggest, is our problem, not curriculum or teaching. Something is essentially wrong with the institution—the church school—itself. Classrooms—schools—may simply not provide the best means by which to communicate the Christian faith or the best places to learn. They most certainly are not a reasonable starting point for our thinking about church education. It is about time we stopped making false starts from erroneous assumptions about the nature of religious education. Schooling ought to be our secondary, not our primary, concern.

No person is born a Christian. He is brought to faith by his experiences with or within the community of Christian faith. At best the bearers of the good news can share their message so that others might experience its reality. The attraction of Christianity from the very beginning was the lives of Christians. It was not as disembodied truth that the Christian "Good News" laid hold of men; it was through the corporate life of the little Christian societies in the cities of the ancient world. Men coming into contact with these communities of faith experienced a new reality. In that way, probably, more than by the preaching of any individuals, the church grew.

Someone has said that Christianity is not taught so much as caught. That was certainly true in the first century. Men had the Christian faith transmitted to them through their experiences with the community of faith. The distinguishing mark of the early church was not its verbal message (words), its preaching and teaching, but its nonverbal message (the Word), its style of life.

The history of the early community of faith is the story of the converting example of Christian lives. It was the "little people," the men and women and children who were ever ready to die for their new life, who carried the good news into the recesses of society. Nameless and despised by the intelligent and cultured and wealthy and important, they lived lives so unique that they attracted other people who wanted to know why they were different. In response they attempted to identify why and interpret how it was possible for them to be living with a new understanding of life and death.

The pagan critic of the early Christians, Celsus, described it this way:

> In private lives we see . . . the most illiterate and bucolic yokels, who would not dare to say anything at all in front of their elders and more intelligent masters. But when they get ahold of those who have been attracted to their living witness . . . they let out some astonishing statement as for example that their fathers and schoolteachers talk nonsense and have no understanding, and that in reality they neither know nor are to do anything good, but are taken up with mere empty chatter. But they alone, they say, know the right way to live and if the children would believe them, they would become happy and make their homes happy as well.[1]

In those disparaging words was the written record of the nature of education in the early church. Somewhere along the way we have forgotten that the communication of the faith takes place in ways that can rightly be identified as education, but not necessarily as classroom instruction.

For the last few years I have been asking members of Christian education committees in local congregations one question: What do you do? Typically they respond: We are responsible for the Sunday church school. . . . With a few variations on that theme, they explain that their church has a nursery and classes for children from preschool through junior high. They help find teachers and things like that. Their minister runs a confirmation class and they have a youth group for high-schoolers and perhaps adult Bible classes. The Christian education committee is responsible for all these activities in the church.

In those churches which some consider to be more progressive the conversation goes further. They talk of being the ones to secure a minister or director of Christian education so as to provide professional leadership for their church school and youth groups. Sometimes they mention their responsibility for the planning and construction of a new building with modern educational facilities and equipment. A few talk about directing weekday classes sponsored ecumenically with professional teachers or the development of new courses of instruction.

To most churchmen the term church education is synonymous with church schooling. In conventional terms one gets a Christian education by going to church school. We therefore improve church education by improving church schools. Christian education committees are obviously responsible for church schools. If a church is concerned about educating their children and youth, they see to it that a school is provided for formal instruction.

Laymen are not the only ones who identify church education with church schooling. Attend a meeting of local church directors of Christian education—the conversation will center on schooling. Read the typical church educational magazine and you find it concerned solely with the church school. Look at the labors of most denominational boards of Christian education and you will see them producing curricular resources for church schools, institutes for teacher education and the like. This concentration on schools leads one to ponder whether it is possible to become educated as a Christian without going through a process of schooling carried out in special institutions designed for that purpose. I think it is. In fact, I contend that this exclusive association of education with schooling is a fateful error. Any church interested in becoming an educating community would be wise to question it.

When Plato talked about education he gave almost no consideration to schools. Instead he affirmed that the community educates through all those forces which influence the mind and character of men.

Thomas Jefferson believed in schooling but it never occurred to him that schooling was or would be the dominant concern of educators. In fact, he attributed a relatively minor role to schools. From Jefferson to Horace Mann to John Dewey, educators understood education as being much broader than schooling.

A few years ago, Lawrence A. Cremin wrote a liberating book, *The Genius of American Education,* in which he explains convincingly that Dewey began his career with the acknowledgment that all of life educates, deliberate education representing only a small part of a person's education. For Dewey, even deliberate education was broader than schooling. It included the influences of home, neighborhood, factory, church, school and other such community institutions.

But when Dewey examined these centers of education he concluded that home, factory, community, and church were not performing adequately their educational responsibilities. Therefore he made his giant leap into an affirmation that the school must assume the total responsibility for the education of children. As Cremin comments, "His decision was a fateful one for American educational theory; for it effectively removed the agencies of informal education from the purview of educators."

I don't think we realize the lingering and pervasive influence of Dewey. We Americans have an almost myopic reaction to all our problems. To counter the Russian advancement in the space race, we immediately responded by developing more physics courses. Desiring to lower our insurance rates, we insisted that schools provide driver education courses. In the fear of our daughter's having children out of wedlock, we initiated courses on the sanctity of marriage. Our anxiety over drugs will surely cause a demand for more courses. Religion courses may even result from our fear of biblical illiteracy. We are conditioned to seek solutions to all our problems in the same manner: we develop a course to be taught in a school, rarely asking what schools are for. I happen to favor courses in physics and sex education but not because of fear. At the same time, however, I do not believe that offering such courses will solve our problems. No good educator does, but some give the impression that they do.

It is probably only natural that we have done the same thing in the church. In a day of anxiety and frustration about the Christian education of children and youth, we hope for a beefed-up church school. We spend large sums of money on new educational plants; we redesign the content to be taught; we develop new curricular resources, and increase the use of new media; we devise methods for teacher education, hire professional leadership, expand our church school programs, and reorganize our school environment. We explore and develop new teaching methods such as individualized instruction, teaching machines, team teaching, ungraded classes, homogeneous grouping, independent study and the like. We try ecumenical schools and weekday classes.

These attempts at reform in church education are not in themselves going to meet our educational needs. What is demanded is a major shift in emphasis from schooling to education, i.e., all the ways a person learns. This does not mean to deny the role of schooling, but it does mean putting it in its proper place as a secondary concern. The consequences of assuming that education primarily or necessarily takes place in schools or should take place in schools have been destructive. This identification must not only be re-examined, but rejected.

If denominations, in response to local requests, continue to spend a major portion of their time, talent and money redesigning the content to be taught in church schools, packaging it in a more interesting and teachable curriculum, increasing resources of new instructional media, suggesting the restructuring of church school environments and the recruiting and training of more talented teachers, they will be ignoring the basic educational needs of our day. To seek such conventional reform of our existing church schools as a major educational goal is less than adequate. If we are concerned about the future of church education, we must aim for a more revolutionary reconsideration of the total context through which the church pursues its educational objectives. It's about time we stopped worrying about church schools and turned our attention to more important matters.

Research which points to the tremendous influence of the environment in which a child lives during his first six years continues to mount. Studies continue to indicate the profound effect of childhood experiences and the effect of the mass media, especially television. There are an increasing number of conclusive articles on the influence of the peer group in the education of youth. We have become much more aware of the impact of forces outside the school which affect the education of persons. To have a myopic view of education as schooling is to miss the significance of the other contexts in which education consciously or unconsciously takes place. Thus we find a growing number of spokesmen for radical reform in education. While most of them agree that the first step is eliminating an identification of schooling and education, one of the most vocal, Ivan Illich, believes that schooling has become a mad religion in the United States. He points out that it is an illusion that the most important learning happens in school and suggests that perhaps the money and resources now expended for schools should be redirected to education in a broader sense. Schooling, Illich explains, is so expensive that it is beyond the greatest hope of two thirds of the people in Latin America. But they are being indoctrinated to believe that unless they can be schooled, they will remain inferior, uneducated persons. He does not understand why North Americans equate education with schooling or why we believe that more schooling makes better citizens. He says that we think about improving or revamping the system of schools when what we need instead is an alternative to schooling. Yet he admits that no matter how inefficient schools are in educating people, it is difficult to get people to see that schools are not necessarily *the* answer to their educational needs.

Obviously we can make some connections between his remarks and church schools in the thousands of our small American churches. Someone has convinced people that if they are concerned about the education of their children and youth they must have a church school. But most of these churches find that the construction of adequate educational plants is almost impossible. Small rooms filled with tables and chairs used only one hour each week are not economical. Moreover, few of these churches can afford professional leadership for their church schools. Talk of movie cameras, TV sets, tape recorders, and computers for programmed instruction jolts the minds of these folk . . . and rightly so. Expensive teacher training institutes and the thought of paid professional teachers overwhelm them. The cost of new curriculum resources strains their already inadequate church budgets. Is this the best use of a church's limited funds? Do these churches really need church schools? I used to believe so but I don't any longer. It is quite possible that a church can develop a program of Christian education without a church school.

There are some who have given up on the church as a learning and witnessing community. I haven't. One night not long ago I found myself in the living room of a suburban home near a small college campus on the West Coast. A young priest, wearing sports clothes, invited me to join him and his congregation for a celebration. These adults, teenagers and children met regularly to celebrate their common faith and life. In the dining room, a long table was set with loaves of bread and bottles of wine, as well as fruit and cheese. The house had a festive atmosphere. Large colorful paper flowers and birds hung from the ceiling. I was greeted with a bag decorated on the outside with large dayglow colors which read, "We Care." Opening the bag, I found a large red and yellow sheet of tissue paper with a hole in the middle and a variety of other things. We each picked a partner to dress in the paper costume We read them part of an E. E. Cummings poem: "I love you most beautiful darling, more than anything on earth, and I like you better than anything in the sky." We fed each other a Hershey Kiss. Together, we stuffed a balloon with confetti, blew it up, tossed it into the air, punctured it with a pin. As the confetti fell over us, we blew party horns. The daily news programs, blaring from the two television sets in the room, were turned down as someone began to strum a guitar. Everyone joined in the folk song "Turn, Turn, Turn" as we made our way to the table.

There we each greeted our neighbor with the ancient kiss of peace. Everyone had a part in the reading of scripture and original brief simple English prayers. We prayed the Lord's Prayer. But following "Thy will be done on earth as it is in heaven," reports from the day's newspaper were read, and we each made our confessions of apathy in the face of need. An offering of money and fair housing pledge cards was made that evening. Each person made a personal affirmation of what he believed. Some were moving: "I believe in God—which is to trust that someone, somewhere, is not stupid." Together we affirmed our understanding of the Christian faith as "Where there is life, there is death, but where there is death there is hope." We acknowledged that with such a perception of life we could affirm the negative aspects of our history as the birth pangs of a new age. Our priest broke the bread and blessed it. He poured the wine and blessed it, each person serving his neighbor. We joined hands and sang joyfully and he concluded with Jesus' words to Simon Peter, "Simon, son of John, do you love me more than all else?" We answered with Peter's words, "Yes, Lord, you know that I love you," and our host responded with Jesus' words, "Then feed my sheep." As we sat at the table to share the bread, cheese, wine, and fruit, we struggled to decide what we must do during the next week about racism in the community and the places where we studied and worked. Two hours later, as a community, we formulated definite resolves for action, sang "We Shall Overcome," and, with the kiss of peace, departed into the night.

The church through its life can educate persons into its faith. But to do so the church must be understood as a witnessing community. It is necessary for the church, and that means congregations, to exhibit a distinctive life style in order to communicate their faith.

Question: What would such an educating community of faith look like?

Let me try to answer that question by suggesting what I would look for. I would look for a community of persons who are actively involved as a political and social force in the world.

I would look for a community that gathers to celebrate a particular and peculiar way of looking at life.

I would look for a community struggling to be a bearer of that frame of reference by seeking ways to give it shape in their own lives and in society.

I would look for a community that is somewhat unique among other human communities, i.e., whose style of life, individual and social, stands out from that of the surrounding culture.

I would look for a community of persons who are disturbed by their own lives and their society—a group painfully engaged in an attempt to become what they know they should be, but are not yet.

I would look for a community with a vision—hope—a community that affirmed a new possibility for men and history.

I would look for a community so grasped by a vision of a new humanity that they could not avoid being involved in attempts to make that vision a reality for all men.

I would look for a community captured by a dream of

a new human society—realizing that dreams only come true when people act to make them do so.

I would look for a community that gathered together only so that it could get straight what it ought to be doing to change the world.

I would look for a group that came together to experiment with what the new humanity might be like.

I would look for a community of faith that gathered together to acquire the power they needed to enter the conflict of God's kingdom building. Such a church would be an educating community, whether or not it had classrooms, teachers, and courses of instruction and curriculum.

No longer do we have to assume that church education requires school classrooms. Education is much broader than schools and much more fundamental than classes. After we loosen ourselves from the constricted position that all education is programmed, planned, and occurs in schools, our imaginations can discover a host of exciting possibilities for learning.

Don't misunderstand. I am not suggesting that schooling should be eliminated. Schools as a context for learning can be important. But it is not the only, or even primary, place for church education. Christian education committees need a broader understanding of their responsibility as well as a greater imagination in planning their educational ministry. I do not want to give the impression that Christian education is everything the church does. However, everything a congregation does or does not do has educational implications. Those responsible for church education cannot afford the false security of compartmentalizing their concerns.

Those who wish to limit church education to instruction in a school classroom have ignored their responsibility. Those who like to live in boxes will be attracted to this kind of thinking which gives everyone a distinct responsibility. But Christian education is not a specific discipline or category in a division of labor. Rather it is a way of approaching or dealing with everything a church does. The arguments which attempt to limit the definition of education and give it a specific "job to do" are wrong and irrelevant. Christian education is not merely one branch of the church's program for every occasion or event is potentially educational. Education occurs when people plan to have something happen or when they become aware of what is happening and respond. It is a mistake to divide up responsibility in the church so that one group is concerned for evangelism (the communication of the faith), one for social action/service (the living out of the faith) and one for education (transmission of the heritage, information about tradition, and skills to apply the faith to everyday life). This division of responsibilities into distinctive tasks may have been in the past a viable way for the church to live but it is no longer so.

What I am suggesting is a radical shift in the way we think about education and the role of those responsible for it. Once we have freed ourselves from identifying church education with church schooling we are on the way toward discovering that new way to look at Christian education.

Now is the time to make a major shift in our thinking from schooling to education. I do not assume that this will be easy, for our total experience up to the present has taught us otherwise.

VII. WHERE WE ARE NOW

Church buildings, budgets, organizations, congregational life-styles, social action and worship are essential aspects of church education. In our Protestant individualism we forget the central importance of communities as places where communication and teaching occur. But as Ellis Nelson in his book *Where Faith Begins* put it: "There is no New Testament book addressed to individuals or to children. Philemon is about an individual, Onesimus; but the burden of that book is how the house church is to receive the runaway slave." [1]

I remember a divinity school student recalling his experience in a congregation. He told me about being brought up in an atheistic home. During his college years certain questions haunted him, questions about the nature of life and death. He felt he had to answer those questions before he could go to medical school. So at the end of his college career he went to a divinity school where he hoped to find answers to his questions. He chose an ecumenical seminary in a university setting, with no intention of going into the ministry. He was in an economic bind since his parents would not support him in this quest. However, at divinity school he discovered that his fellow students were getting jobs in churches. He chose to work with youth in a church which offered the highest salary. Today, as he looks back on his motive, he recognizes it as questionable. But at the time what impressed him was that no one ever asked him what he believed or seemed interested in the kind of person he was. He was sure that if they had questioned him on either of those matters they would not have hired him. From his point of view they represented a community of people who, though he thought he was unacceptable, accepted him. Until then most of his life had been spent earning the respect of his parents, colleagues, friends and teachers. All of a sudden here was a group of people who took him in on a different basis.

That experience by itself might not have had a tremendous effect, but it was followed by another revealing incident. One evening at a meeting of over 100 high school youth, two boys were making popcorn in the kitchen. One of them shouted from the kitchen something about putting salt in the popcorn. The other made it clear that he didn't agree. The voices rose until a loud noise interrupted the argument. Through a wooden door came the body of one of the boys. In the resulting confusion, both of them disappeared, leaving him with 100 very upset teenagers. They were angry because as they put it, these two boys had done nothing but destroy everything that they enjoyed since kindergarten. He confessed that he didn't know how to handle the situation so they sat down to talk about it. The conversation went late into the evening. Before the last ones left, the group had decided to contribute to repairing the door and to ask the fellows back to make popcorn next week (in two bowls, one with salt and one without). He said he would always remember that discussion about giving people what they need, not what they deserve.

Another night, sitting in Paul Tillich's apartment, he listened to him talk about the Christian faith as the good news—that man is accepted though unacceptable. Those words identified and interpreted his two impressive experiences in a local congregation and helped him to make a major decision. He would join the church and enter the Christian ministry.

I've seen that young man since. Unfortunately, he is no longer participating in the life of a congregation. Regretfully, he discovered that his two experiences in that particular congregation were an exception and not the rule.

The experiences people have or do not have in the faith community (the church) are the key to whether or not they will be grasped by the faith or whether or not it will have any meaning for them. The life style of the faith community communicates.

In a nursery school class of four-year-olds, I watched a teacher moving from free play to group time. She sang a little song about when you're through with your toys put them away. She came to Johnny and said, "Johnny, would you help me put your blocks away?" "No," he replied. She smiled at him: "Johnny, some days I feel like that myself. Today I'll help you and maybe tomorrow you'll help me." Johnny watched her put his blocks away. She finished and turned away. He picked up a block and threw it at her. She stopped, turned around, took Johnny in her arms. "Johnny," she said, "I know you're angry at me and there's nothing wrong with that. But I can't let you hurt anybody. We all have to learn to talk with our mouths and not with our hands. I want to hold you till we both feel better about ourselves."

In a few moments Johnny stopped screaming and relaxed. She let him go to join the other children. Johnny went off by himself to play. Slowly he worked himself back toward the group, plopped himself in her lap, interrupted her story, and exclaimed, "I like you."

As I understand it, Johnny experienced what the faith community calls reconciliation. Someday if someone identifies or interprets that experience as reconciliation Johnny will understand. Providing experience which corresponds to words ought to be a major concern of the church as an educating community. For better or worse church education takes place through the life styles of Christian communities.

Less obvious, but just as crucial for education in the local church, is its budget. It is a theological statement of faith far more powerful than those recited on Sunday morning. It is more than a way of dividing up our economic resources to pay our operating costs. A budget is solidified beliefs.

But when do we as church educators attend a finance committee meeting at our church? Do we know how decisions on our budget are made? If we have attended such meetings did we find persons struggling to determine the educational implications of their budgetary decisions? Do we often ask whether we should spend our money to repair the church organ or use it to begin a community day care center? Has our Christian education committee ever considered that the church budget falls within their purview and responsibility? Why not?

Consider questions such as these: What do the salaries we pay our church employees communicate about the value of persons? What does the amount we spend on personal needs as compared to that we set aside for the church's mission in the world say about the primary reasons for the existence of our congregation? What does the amount of money we make available to our social action committee and the amount set aside for flowers and music communicate about our primary concerns? What does the proportion we spend on church education and on office expenses tell about our priorities? What does our avoidance of taxes say about the church's involvement in community life? What does the percentage spent for church buildings and the percentage spent on people and programs say about our understanding of the church?

If we have ever asked such questions, we have probably discovered that most of us don't like to talk about money in such terms. Maybe we ought to try to, for money is an affirmation of faith. To understand what a person thinks, look at how he spends his money. To find out if someone believes in your cause, ask him for a significant contribution.

I can imagine a finance committee calling a church meeting to address the issue of reparations to the black community and making a proposal that their church remortgage its total plant and give that money without strings to a black church or business enterprise. The agonizing process of dealing with this issue would help a church comprehend the educational dimensions of its budget.

I can therefore imagine a finance committee and a Christian education committee planning to involve their congregation in a discussion of their charitable endeavors. At present we tend to think of charity as the contribution of money for the sake of the deprived, a pattern which goes back to the ancient practice of almsgiving. It is still the practice of most churches, women's fellowships, youth groups, and even denominations, but it is not a practice to be accepted without question.

Arthur McGill in an unpublished paper entitled "Problems Facing the Church" explained that monetary giving may be outmoded and unnecessary, an irresponsible form of charity. Why? Because governmental agencies can do the job better. He points out that in 1967 the largest almsgiving type of operation, the United Fund, raised six hundred million dollars. In contrast, state governments spent almost eight billion on welfare and that was only 15 percent of their total budgets. The United States government spent almost twelve billion in projects of the Department of Health, Education and Welfare and that was only 8 percent of the total national budget. He points out that such funding makes private charity quite irrelevant. The church must find new ways to participate in charity. He suggests that the church turn to political endeavors which will affect government spending and the decisions of government welfare agencies. McGill writes: "For the individual and the Christian community the days of charity by the gift are over. The days of charity by the vote and political pressure group have begun." He has posed an issue which ought to be debated. Questions of budgets and economics are the responsibilities of church educators because they result in program and program reveals our theology. The way we spend our time and money teaches what we believe. It's about time we took them more seriously as educational concerns.

Buildings, like budgets, are also solidified ideas. They are important to the church's educational ministry, not because they provide a place for church school classes but because they communicate the faith of those who own and use them. It is difficult to teach about humility in a congregation that spends a great deal of its time, energy and money building a status symbol on the village green. Sermons on brotherhood have little meaning in congregations that keep their church property locked up for their private weekly use.

Stories for children on Christian concern for the poor do not make much sense in a church which spends thousands of dollars to build a church school plant for use one hour each week while refusing to consider the construction of low-cost housing in the empty lot owned by the church. Statements about the church's concern for youth make little impact in a church which builds expensively furnished church parlors so that ladies can hold high teas, but denies the construction of a youth coffee house or discotheque where young people can discuss draft resistance. Congregations who want to communicate to the world that they possess a faith relevant and meaningful to contemporary man don't communicate very well when they build new buildings of colonial or Gothic design. Neither expresses a modern idiom or makes possible contemporary worship. It is also true that prayers which ask God to help the poor seem to lack meaning for a group of twenty-five gathered in a large old ornate structure (which consumes the major part of their economic resources) in which they refuse to raise the question: Do we need a church building to be a community of faith?

My point should be clear. Church buildings and their use are related to the church's educational ministry. I recall the First International Congress on Religion, Architecture, and the Visual Arts—especially an address by Dr. J. G. Davies, director of the Institute for the Study of Worship and Religious Architecture at the University of Birmingham, England. He began with the assertion that the church had only one function: service. A church, before it considers building, ought to ask about the needs of all those who live in the area that surrounds it. He envisioned churches as multi-purpose buildings to serve the needs of the community and he was critical of those buildings which were established as sacred shrines or as worship stations to serve the privatized needs of church members. Davies could not understand a separation of the sacred and the secular. He could not envision special buildings which "looked like" churches. He only understood buildings for the service of men, buildings in which men could encounter, as he put it, "the God of history acting in the world today." Churches ought to be practical, inexpensive buildings which can serve the needs of people. Churches, he suggested, might be designed to last for only a few years. When the needs of people in the area change, new buildings can be constructed to meet new needs. Just picture how much easier it would be to rethink church education if church school plants constructed during the building boom of a few years ago had a life span of ten years.

The least we should do is rethink the use of our church school buildings. Perhaps a huge church school edifice in a city church could be made over into apartments for young adults. In the suburbs they might be loaned to the public school system so as to avoid a new building program. In the country they could serve as offices for a variety of social service and welfare organizations. It would be well for us to question what our buildings communicate and how they might become better allies in our educational ministry.

Another aspect of education in the church, as neglected as budgets and buildings, is its organization. We communicate through organizational structure. Since time is a valuable commodity, the ways we ask a person to use his time says something important about our values. How a church is organized shows how it expects its people to use their time and talents. When we organize a church in ways which require our leaders to spend their time at committees and boards which serve the private needs of the congregation, then we are saying to them, this is the mission of the church. On the other hand, if we ask them to give their free time to task forces which are engaged in dealing with the social issues which face their community, nation and world, then we're saying that these are the mission of the church and the concern of its ministry.

Christian education potentially occurs whenever Christians gather for worship, for work, and action; it is a by-product of the congregation's life style. Unless we begin to look at education from this broader perspective, we will discover that it is difficult for the church to be an educating community.

Why is it that we so rarely question the organizational structures of our churches? Each year a nominating committee assumes the painful task of finding live bodies to fill the openings on its boards and committees. We do so unconsciously, rarely asking any questions.

I once found myself in a new organization which, following the usual pattern, elected at its first meeting a president, vice-president, secretary and treasurer. Two months later we discovered we didn't intend to have a treasury, we didn't need minutes and we really didn't want a president. All we wanted was a chairman. In the same way, it is typical American behavior to form committees to sit down and discuss every issue which concerns us. The church which does the same rarely evaluates the effectiveness of their activity or disbands them. Instead we multiply them. At some point we discover that we have more committees than available leadership so we put the same persons on more than one committee. Eventually we have our most creative, resourceful leadership tied up in five nights of church committee meetings each week to carry out business which could be handled better in other ways. The saddest aspect of this picture is our belief that we have an active church because so many of our people are busy in it.

Many of our organizational structures are based upon needs that no longer exist. Some work against the church's becoming a learning and witnessing faith community.

I would suggest that we make a functional, diagrammatic sketch of our church's organizational structure. That is, a diagram which shows the number of man-hours and money spent on each board, committee and group as well as what each one accomplishes. It might shock us to ask: According to our diagram, how and where does our church educate people to use their time and talent as churchmen? What does our church's present organizational structure teach the world about the nature and function of the church? How might we reorganize for a more effective ministry?

Don't misunderstand me. I do not assume that the restructuring of a church will solve all its problems or make it a more effective educating community. But I do believe that if we look critically at our organization we might discover whether or not it enables us to fulfill our mission in the world.

Church organization must be continually judged as to its effectiveness. By and large over the past fifty years there has been little change in the bureaucracy of local churches. Most changes have been for efficiency rather than effectiveness. For example, we add a church council which serves to keep everyone informed about what everyone else is doing rather than seeking the most effective way for the church to be a change agent in the community.

In most churches we compartmentalize our ministry. We have a Christian education committee which assumes that their major responsibility is the organization of a church school; missionary committees attempt to raise benevolence budgets; social action committees talk about social problems; finance committees prepare budgets; boards of trustees control the use of the building; boards of deacons are responsible for worship services. But all of these concerns have educational dimensions. Perhaps what we need is a series of short-lived task forces to address particular issues such as racism. Such task forces could engage the whole faith community in congregational meetings to act and reflect on their life and work. Such congregational meetings could spawn forth new task forces to meet new issues. In every case the time, talent and economic resources of the community of faith would be directed toward action in the community on those issues. Certainly there are numerous household and support functions which are a necessary part of any organization or institution. My point is that these need to be kept in proper perspective.

That brings us to one last dimension of the church's educational ministry: worship. If we ask most Christian education committees or church educators about worship they immediately think of the church school, and begin to talk about ways of conducting "opening or closing exercises" for children before or after classes. Our conversation quickly turns to the need for more worship helps and resources. Many superintendents feel that conducting what they call worship services for children is their major responsibility. They're not sure what worship means. They know they don't have much time to prepare to lead it, and want someone to do it for them, i.e., give them an outline of a service, tell them what songs to sing and give them a story to tell. Someday someone is going to be brave enough to suggest to them that they might be wasting their time. These church school services often work against everything the church hopes to accomplish in its educational ministry. Much of what children learn by participating in them is perhaps negative.

I suggest that children belong with adults in the celebrations of the community of faith. If the liturgy of the church isn't relevant to children then it ought to be changed. Worship should be a celebration of all the people in the faith community together. Something important is missed when children do not share their experience with the total congregation.

But I am also much concerned about the educational dimensions of the church's worship, something Protestants have rarely considered. When we mention education and worship many ministers think of the sermon. Increasingly the sermon is an inadequate means of education. On occasion one can learn from a lecture. Although some lecturers do teach, there are so few good lectures that most people do not learn from them. To assume that a sermon in the middle of the service is a teaching tool can be misleading. Even in universities, where professors still lecture, there are opportunities for discussion and question asking. I have the feeling that except for a few rare occasions, the sermon might be eliminated from the weekly service. Perhaps then we would be able to understand how the liturgy itself teaches.

I recall a youth group that tried to understand the nature of worship. They worked long and hard. The "offering" gave them the most trouble. They came to the conclusion that the offering provided an opportunity for persons symbolically to act out their commitment by dedicating themselves to particular action. The offering then

Where We Are Now 77

was the highlight of the celebration, coming after the congregation had heard the gospel and before they went into the world or gathered around the table to share the supper of the kingdom in which they were committed to live. But when the young people looked at their own church's worship service they had some problems. The first thing that bothered them was that the place of the offering in the service didn't make sense. It seemed to come at a point when the choir needed a chance to sing. They had a lot of other problems with this part of the service. Yet talking about what the offering meant, gave them an idea. In a few weeks the church was to take a special offering in behalf of racial justice. In the past this had meant that an envelope was sent to every home to be returned and placed in the Sunday offering plate. The youth weren't sure the congregation took this act very seriously. Some accused their parents of hypocrisy. As one put it, "A small gift for racial justice each year gets my father off the hook. He doesn't really want racial justice." They devised what they believed to be a better plan. Why not send everyone in the church a fair housing pledge card, let every family talk it over at home. When the time came to make an offering for racial justice, they could bring their signed cards and place them on the altar as a symbolic commitment to action. This would be a dramatic act of faith by a community and a sign of the kingdom whose coming was to be celebrated with the bread and wine that followed.

Unfortunately the official board of that church never accepted their idea. As a result a number of young people left the church, at least for the time and, perhaps, forever. I wonder whether we understand the educational dimension of the offering and the other aspects of the worship service.

So far we have been talking about worship as the celebration of the community of faith. But we should remember that when Paul was asked the question, "What is reasonable worship?" he did not answer by suggesting orders of worship, hymns, sermons, prayers, or celebration activities. He replied, "Present your bodies as a living sacrifice," and then he went on to clarify what he meant by outlining what we would call social action programs.

All of life, including what we call social action, is the worship of God, an offering to God. The way we live each day should reflect what we celebrate in the faith community.

It seems clear that children and youth can learn about worship only as they participate actively in the total life of a congregation. No longer can we afford to ignore the educational implications of every aspect of our life in a congregation. The community of faith educates best and most significantly through the experiences we offer to persons to share in our life. The future of relevant church education is with those who take seriously experience in the life of a congregation. Here is the place to begin as we plan for the church becoming an educating community.

VIII. NEVER TOO EARLY

A question: When does Christian education begin? A typical answer: When children go to school—first grade. A wiser reply: The moment a child is born.

While a growing number of churches offer classes for three-, four-, and five-year-olds, most adults think of them as baby sitting centers; places to keep their children safe and busy while they attend church functions. Some parents take these preschool classes more seriously, demanding that their children be taught the Bible instead of being permitted to play. Both groups are misguided. More than baby sitting is demanded, but trying to teach Bible stories and prayers is a mistake. Church education for the preschool years is the most important education we provide. It is education of a special kind; it is education for children and adults; it is education which begins at birth. Do you believe that? I do.

A rapidly growing mass of research supports earlier hypotheses that the first three years are the crucial years in the life of every human being. We are now convinced that the environment in which a child lives during his earliest years is a major determinant of his personality and future behavior. If we are really concerned about the growth of persons we had better place a major emphasis on the very early years of a child's life.

For years psychoanalysts have been saying loud and clear that the attitudes formed in infancy are crucial for later life. Erik Erikson has been preaching that basic trust, which is the ground of all later trust, depends upon the first few years. (Our religious affections themselves are a result of early childhood experiences.) Each of us is more a result of our earliest experiences than our later experiences.

Up to the present we may have lacked significant evidence for these claims. Now we have it. One source is the research of Benjamin Bloom, published under the title *Stability and Change in Human Characteristics*.[1]

He discovered, for example, that our success in reading is dependent upon early childhood experiences. Those whose early years provided them with convictions that reading was valuable, and who had acquired trust in themselves and their abilities, learned to read easily. Conversely those who had little trust in themselves and their abilities and lacked a conviction that reading was valuable had difficulty in learning to read.

Bloom found that the characteristics acquired early in life are the most stable. Thus while a person may change, it becomes increasingly difficult with each ensuing year to facilitate that change. He also established that basic personality and behavioral characteristics are essentially formed during the early years and that these become more stable as time goes on. His study indicated that the outward manifestations of those basic stable characteristics may change, but that directing our attention to these outward manifestations (for example, drug use, violent behavior, etc.) only changes the symptom and not the characteristics which underlie them.

The psychiatrist Bruno Bettelheim has discussed the implications of Bloom's findings on a number of occasions. He, too, is convinced that the behavior, values, attitudes and beliefs of youth today have their basis in early childhood experiences. He points out that too many parents bring up their children through a series of contradictions, all of which make no sense. We tell a child, "This is your room," but then we make him keep it and his possessions the way we adults want it. The conflicting difference between what we say and what we do seems to help to produce youth who feel that our society makes little sense and regard those over thirty as difficult to trust. The early years are the formative years.

Studies continue to pile up data on the crucial nature of the first three years of life. For example, the extent to which a boy will demonstrate aggressive behavior is more or less fixed by the time he is three. And when a mother attends to a child in distress as soon as he cries, it leads the child to believe there is something he can do. He learns that he can have an effect upon the world.

To read the research of behavioral scientists is like reading this piece of free verse by Dorothy Law Nolte:

> If a child lives with criticism
>   He learns to condemn
> If a child lives with hostility
>   He learns to fight
> If a child lives with ridicule
>   He learns to be shy
> If a child lives with jealousy
>   He learns to feel guilty
> If a child lives with tolerance

He learns to be patient
If a child lives with encouragement
He learns confidence
If a child lives with praise
He learns to appreciate
If a child lives with fairness
He learns justice
If a child lives with security
He learns to have faith
If a child lives with approval
He learns to like himself
If a child lives with acceptance and friendship
He learns to find love in the world.[2]

All this research points to the need for the church's playing a much larger role in early childhood education than it now does. But before churches can assume a more significant role they will have to take a critical look at their present programs. In many cases what they are now doing is detrimental. Sometimes preschool education in the church works against the concerned parent. I have saved the following letter to remind me of that.

Dear John,

We have some beautiful times at home. I stretch out on the floor and read *Suzuki Beane* to the kids while they crawl all over me and we talk about how the Endsville that Suzuki and Henry made is the way everybody ought to live—"Where a square can be a square and a swinging cat can really swing. And kids can feel things because they do." And we play "The Red Balloon" on the record player and talk about being only children and how it feels when your balloon breaks or when the "big kids" pick on you. Jill picked up the word "divinity" from the school and we decided it was the same thing as "supercalifragilisticex-pialadoceous."

So many good things happen—except on Sunday. I tried

things like this on Sunday at church school and the kids loved it. But I only succeeded in getting myself voted out at annual meeting because, "You're supposed to go to Sunday school to read the Bible, not to play games." And I don't care what kind of stamina you think you have or how much you may believe in what you're doing, something dies inside when you realize what's happening.

I think this week we have hit the ultimate low in Christian education. Let me explain and see if perhaps it is just that I am super-sensitive about what's happening to our kids. I've talked with a couple of people and I get the remark, "Well, it's just for a week of vacation Bible school."

The first day Jill (she's five) came home and said, "We made a picture today and I made the biggest dandelion in the whole world and made a folder and we have to keep all the pictures in them and we can't bring them home and I wanted to show you my picture 'cause I made it for a surprise for you." All one breath and a big flood of tears. I have a thing about my kids; every time they cry I do, too. So we cried and had lunch and took a nap, and the minute Jill woke up she wanted to go back to church and get that picture. We walked over and I peeked into the folder, but we left the dandelion there alone with no one to admire it. The same thing happened on Tuesday except that Jill wouldn't eat any supper Tuesday night because the kitten she'd made was all alone at the church. I couldn't stand it any longer so I told her it was all right—if she made the picture it was hers and she could do what she wanted to with it.

Wednesday morning the teacher came and said to me: "I have a problem with Jill. She said you told her she could do what she wanted with her picture because she made it."

"Yes, that's what I told her."

"Well, why should she be different than all the other

kids? I told them they had to leave them here until Friday."

"I know you told them, but I maintain a child has a right to be an individual."

"Well, if you want her to be an individual why don't you put her in a class by herself? She also told me she was going to make a rabbit that was as big as hell. I suppose you think that's cute?"

Meantime, Jill was standing there crying and saying over and over, "But, Mommy, I wanted to surprise you each day."

I know the teacher is saying that she'd like to have something to show at the end of the week. I hear it and in turn know something about her. And, yes, I do think a big-as-hell rabbit is cute. Probably she learned it from me anyway.

So Jill and I came home and talked. Jill decided that the teacher was "fresh," and I said I was sure the teacher thought we were, too. Then we played the "orchestra record" and pretended Jill was the flute with the high little voice and Mommy was the clarinet with the middle voice and the teacher was the saxophone with the loud voice. Each one had its own song and they were all pretty, but they were a lot more interesting when they all played together. Then we listened to the whole thing and I think Jill knows that sometimes it really is time to play your own song, but there are other times when everyone plays together, and there are even times when the flute echoes the other parts.

Three of Jill's pictures are home now and two are still at the church. Jill is happy, the teacher isn't, and at the moment, I feel like the conductor rehearsing all the instruments that refuse to harmonize. It's so hard to know what to do.

I'm not suggesting that all preschool education in the

church is detrimental. In fact my experience suggests the opposite. Some of the best church educational resources are for three-, four-, and five-year-olds. Some of the most excitingly relevant education is found in church preschool classes where teachers use those resources. But those classes are only one hour a week. If churches are going to take the early childhood years seriously, they will need to expand their educational program to include major commitments of time, talent, and money for adult and preschool education. To do so will demand a shift in priorities.

While the church has put its meager but major emphasis on schooling from first through eighth grade, it seems that it should have been putting its emphasis on young children (birth through five years of age) and correspondingly on adults. Gabriel Moran in *Vision and Tactics: Toward an Adult Church* [3] suggests that the Roman Catholic Church made a similar error by placing all its emphasis on the parochial school. He asserts that early childhood education in the family and adult education ought to be the primary foci of church education. I agree. Parents, he asserts, educate not by being teachers but by being parents. That implies, he points out, a major shift in educational priorities and resources. The burden of his argument and book rests on the conviction that the church must turn its attention to the education of adults.

What the church is called upon to develop is a major experiential program of education for adults and their young children. At one very important point in our lives my wife and I were involved in such a program offered by a college laboratory preschool. When we went to enroll our three-year-old, we discovered that there was going to be more to it than just paying to have her attend nursery school a few days a week. First, it was made clear that children should begin at age three and attend regularly for three years. Sessions ran a full day for five days a week. All the three-, four-, and five-year-old children in a family should attend. Every parent whose child attended the school was to become involved in the program.

We were invited to weekly sessions with the staff of the school to discuss early childhood education and family life. These sessions dealt with the first six years. The school attempted through a variety of means, including social gatherings and lectures, to provide a supportive community for us. The staff was aware that we parents needed to know that we were not alone in our particular approach to child rearing.

We were expected to spend numerous hours observing —through one-way screens—the behavior of our children and their teachers. Conferences followed these observations so that questions could be asked and implications drawn for our behavior at home. We were also expected to participate as teachers' helpers. They knew that we had to have first-hand experiences. We needed to try out our theories and be evaluated on our behavior. In preparation for that responsibility, we were encouraged to read and then participate in simulation experiences with other parents and staff members.

The school's director knew that adult education was an important, if not the most important, part of their program. School and home together had to have the same understanding of child development and offer the same kinds of experiences. In the same way, church, school, and home need to provide complementary and supportive learning environments for young children.

Of course such a major program of early childhood education will call for a significant commitment of time, money and energy. But what is at stake are the lives of children. The difficulties many of us have in becoming fully human can be traced to our early childhood experience. Many of the problems we cause or are unable to cope with in society are a result of the ways some of us were raised. War and peace, poverty and welfare, racism and justice are issues which demand our action. Yet the values, attitudes, beliefs and behavior we bring to deal with these issues all have been influenced by our experiences in those preschool years. If we are to have a society where all men can become fully human, we will have to make a major commitment to early childhood education. Since that involves the relationship of adults with children, a major commitment to adult education will have to be mounted. Certainly it will be costly.

I obviously do not count the cost. And I am convinced the church has the resources for the task if it decides that it is of importance. But there is more than money and personnel involved. We will have to reconsider the family itself, for the family is changing. Increasingly we find one-parent families, and families in which both parents work. We need to consider new models for raising children. Perhaps a group of families can live together and provide a community in which child rearing is shared. Perhaps two parents will divide their time between working and being with the children rather than leaving that task primarily to the mother. Perhaps the church or community will provide the centers for raising children, assuming that role on behalf of the parents. The church ought to play a major role in the development of various new models, for under any conditions the early childhood years are crucial for the growth of persons. We ought now to be exploring the nature of healthy environments for the growth of children under five, seeing that they are established to serve every child in every community.

IX. ALTERNATIVES

Now for the real heresy! I do not recall attending church school as a child. Maybe I didn't. My children have never done so. I do not believe that their Christian education has been neglected. It isn't that I am unconcerned. I continue to struggle with the problem of Christian education, my children and church schooling. Although I cannot find enough significance in one hour a week of classroom instruction to make church schools important for me or my family, still I am committed to the importance of learning in church education.

Therefore let me try to outline my thinking to date. First, I firmly believe that churches need to plan weekday preschool learning centers for three-, four-, and five-year-olds like the ones described in the last chapter.

Second, I believe churches should consider eliminating entirely their present Sunday church school classes for children from grades one through six. Perhaps that sounds extreme. However, there are numerous reasons for suggesting such a conclusion. I find little evidence which indicates that classroom instruction during these childhood years is essential for religious growth or maturity. Children do not appear to be ready to deal with or understand most religious concepts during these years. Too much too soon may not only be without value and a waste of time, but may also prolong childish thinking or make understanding more difficult later.

True, churches have attempted to make these years of schooling into significant classroom experiences by combining religious experience with identification and interpretation. But in spite of many curricular resources for such a task, few church schools seem able to be anything more than an attempt to give children information which they are not interested in possessing. Perhaps the church school classroom model as we know it is our problem. I think so. Therefore let's begin to think about church education during these formative years by thinking of other learning possibilities.

Too often we forget that learning is something which happens inside the learner. In fact, learning is primarily controlled by the learner. A person learns what he wants, when he wants, in the way he wants. Teaching at its best is assisting people to do their own learning. A child is naturally curious. He wants to understand himself and his environment and to make sense out of things. Often we prevent him from learning by the ways we teach. Learning cannot be imposed from the outside. It takes place through personal participation and involvement.

What I am suggesting once more is that learning is a result of experience. We become responsible by assuming responsibility. We do not change our behavior by being told to do so. Information is never enough. We learn by doing. To take these insights seriously is to break away from the classroom model of education.

As we saw in a previous chapter, learning is at its best when it is a collaborative process. While it is personal, it is not individualistic. Each of us has his own style of learning but we learn, grow and mature together.

Today, as a great deal of stress is being put on instructional media and curricular resources, it would be well to remember that the richest resource for learning is the learner himself. A person learns best when what is to be learned is relevant to his needs, and we begin to understand the importance of making people and not courses the basis for education for young people.

Each of us is a thinking and feeling person. The mind does not function separately from the emotions. Emotional as well as intellectual needs must be met. People need to feel respected and accepted, they need to feel they can make mistakes, express their most personal feelings and ideas. They need to understand that what is to be learned is not external to them.

And last, learning is a slow, evolutionary process. There is no need to panic and fear that unless a child learns something or everything right now he never will. Each person learns at his own rate as well as in his own way.

The child is naturally a thinking, acting, feeling, learning animal and we do not need to force him to learn. What we need to do is bring as much of the world as we can into his learning environment, offering as much guidance and assistance as he asks for or needs.

The business of education ought to be the lives of children, and the relationships between children and children, children and adults. Education is not preparation for later life but concern for the present lives of persons. Nothing, no curriculum, content, teacher, schedule or anything else is more important than the learner. Learning at its best is an opportunity for ongoing relationships between children and adults. Let's consider some learning possibilities.

A congregation might organize a number of house

churches. Each of these could become a learning center, bringing together regularly a few families. Once a month and on special days like Christmas, Easter, Pentecost, they might join other such groups for worship. They might (and probably would) participate on occasion in the social action program of their congregation. Most of the time they would go it on their own.

Let me tell you about one. Each week it meets on an appropriate evening, often Friday, at someone's home. There are eight adults and seven elementary school children in this house church. Many of the fathers are away a good deal. And even when they are at home for dinner, none of them arrive till 6:30 P.M. The mothers and children gather around 4:30 to make supper and prepare for the evening. They created a brief candle-lighting service modeled after that used in many Jewish homes on the eve of the Sabbath. This act celebrates their coming together and asks for their fathers' safe return.

When the men arrive, it's supper time. They gather around the table and begin their evening meal, which they set in the context of an original liturgy. It has many of the characteristics of the ancient love feast. Everyone participates. There are times when someone reads and times for silence and times for singing. The event is very contemporary and it celebrates their understanding of the Christian faith.

Following supper they gather around the fireplace in the living room to discuss a community issue. One evening I remember went like this: On a previous occasion they had all decided that racism in their community and schools should be their chief concern for the year. This evening the discussion centered around the hiring of a black teacher. There had never been a black teacher in their school and it looked as if once again a black teacher was going to be denied the "opportunity" to teach their children. The superintendent and school board wanted to keep the issue quiet.

Everyone joined in the discussion about what they might do. One father said, "Why not go to the school board meeting Monday evening and confront them with the issue?" "Let's call the newspaper first so we can get some publicity," commented another. The enthusiasm grew until another father spoke. "Wait a minute, gang (speaking to their children). You have to help us decide. If we go and do this on Monday night, you are all apt to have a rough time in school on Tuesday. Are you willing to have us do it?" The children thought a moment. A second grader piped up. "Do it. It's right. What do you think we are—little kids? We'll take care of them." Everyone laughed. They joined hands and sang a couple of freedom songs together and all went home. I stayed a moment with my host. I asked him, "What if your son had said that he wasn't willing to pay the price of your action? What if he said that he didn't want you to do that? What would you have said or done?" His answer came back quickly, "I thought of that. I would have told him that as a Christian I had to do it. But that I would stay home from work on Tuesday so that when he came home after school I could share his hurt and support him." That's a sample of the kind of learning I think we ought to provide for children from six through eleven years of age. However, that kind of education, as with the preschool centers I have suggested, will demand a prior emphasis on adult education.

For those churches not prepared to support such endeavors there are other possibilities. Not long ago I visited a church which had freed itself from past images of church schooling for elementary school children. Blessed by a fire which destroyed their church school and with a minister who was unwilling to have them reconstruct a building without some serious thought, they worked at building a one room "non-school." With one large room now available they turned to the children to find out what they wanted to do. Some wanted a place to play, some a place to study and discuss things, some a place to create things, some a place to be quiet and alone, some a place to be with their parents so they could do things together. The adults wanted a place to experience celebration and community, where meaningful relationship among different ages and kinds of people could be established, and children's questions could be answered.

The one large room holds a hundred persons, about the size of their congregation. The room has two tiers. The carpeted upper tier has a library for individual study and reading, a place for small groups to view films or listen to records, comfortable areas to sit and talk and a quiet meditation area. The lower level with a concrete floor has fountains in the corners and a large aquarium dividing the space. There is an arts and crafts center on one side and a large open construction area on the other. When I visited in this space children and adults were building a Palestinian home.

A large glass door looks out on a garden play area. Animals roam about, there is a garden to tend, a pool to play in, a sand pile, a tree house and the like. There are no permanent walls inside or out but all the space is divided by beautiful art pieces created by the people themselves with the help of a sculptor. On a typical Sunday morning they simply gather and have fun learning together. Adults and children experience fellowship. They do things together. They ask questions and seek answers. As the minister put it: "We are not anxious to have a traditional school for these children. We don't want to pour information into their heads. The community is the message. We believe that the way we teach is going to influence what we teach. We are trying to find ways to live out the meaning of our faith community and its memory." [1]

I like that idea. Any church could do it, especially small rural churches. There are no teachers (in the traditional sense), no fixed individual classrooms and no worries about how to divide children into classes when there is only one second grader. There is no curriculum material to buy. It is an idea for city churches as well. I know one that meets Friday afternoon and evenings. It is a church with a great many elderly people who live alone and many one-parent families with working mothers. The children come after school. There are choirs, drama, art, and dance groups for them to participate in as well as discussion groups for those interested, and even a tutoring program for those that need such help. Everyone else arrives for pot luck supper. After supper there is some kind of total group activity and sometimes small discussion groups.

The possibilities for church education are unlimited once you free yourself from thinking you need numerous church school classrooms with teachers, pupils, and lessons. The opportunities are so unlimited that I want to dream a moment. My dream was inspired by George Leonard's book *Education and Ecstasy.*[2] Whether or not Leonard presents a utopian dream only time will tell. What he does do is provide a good critique of education as it exists, points to what he means by good education and thereby blows your mind free to construct new educational models. He has his own model. Translated for church it might look like this.

Picture a community where the churches plan an ecumenical center for elementary age children. The center (perhaps in an existing church educational plant) would be open after school every day and on weekends. Staffed by trained church educators, it would provide a variety of learning possibilities. One room might be a canteen. Here children could gather to eat and talk and listen to music. There might be a conversation room, a music room, a multi-media library where children could individually or in groups watch television, movies or filmstrips, where they could read books or listen to records and tapes. There could be a room where children who were interested could individually participate in individual programmed learning. There might be a question-asking room where they could go to seek help, a creative arts room, an action conference room where people would meet to plan action and service projects for their community. There could also be a silent meditation room. There could be a room for meeting people from outside the community so as to hear about their needs and problems first-hand. There might be a game room where situations could be simulated so they could get some understanding of other aspects of life outside their own experience. The possibilities for this ecumenical learning center for children are without limit. Many of our large, now empty, city church school plants could be remodeled into such learning centers on an ecumenical basis.

All three of these suggestions are based upon the belief that people learn what they want most to know, not what we want them to know. People learn when they want to learn and not when we think they ought to learn. They learn in highly personal ways and not according to any particular way we might like them to learn. One thing seems clear, they learn best through participation, action and involvement. All that we can do is make a variety of learning situations available to children and be around to help them learn what they want when they want, in the way they want. We must take seriously these principles as we plan for the future of church education with elementary school children. The first step is to break out of our church school-classroom-instruction mindset. I simply do not believe that church schooling, as we have known it, is the answer for church education during these childhood years.

The church school for an hour a week with volunteer, untrained teachers using a curriculum in a classroom will never provide quality church education. But to maintain such church schools only gives a congregation false security and the erroneous impression that quality church education is being provided. My suggestion is that we eliminate church school classes for elementary age children. Then we will be free to explore alternative learning possibilities. I've suggested three. There are others.

Now to youth. The junior-senior high years are of paramount importance for church education. The basis for education of youth was described in the chapters on action study and issue-centeredness. A variety of learning options should be offered. Opportunities need to be created for bringing youth and adults together so as to explore and search for understanding, meaning and relevance—to share in attempts at problem solving, decision making, and action around issues that concern them in the light of the Christian faith.

I can imagine a group of youth exploring what it means to think theologically. They might begin by identifying an issue in their community with which they believe their congregation should deal. Discovering that it would take two weeks to call a church meeting and believing that the issue should be addressed immediately, they might speak up at the Sunday worship service and thereby confront the congregation with the issue.

During the discussion of the issue by the congregation and the subsequent handling of the situation by the minister and officials of the congregation, these youth would act as passive observers recording how the adults in the church dealt with and reflected upon the issue. After having gathered this information they could withdraw to evaluate the nature of the congregation's action and reflection. Most likely they would discover that the adults did not demonstrate an ability to relate the heritage of the Christian faith to a practical social issue; i.e., they were unable to think theologically. Their next step would be an attempt to discover what theological reflection on such an issue might look like. Once they had made some progress on that problem, they would devise a strategy to teach the adults in their church what they had come to know. Perhaps they would confront the congregation with another issue, but this time actively demonstrate their newly acquired ability to think theologically. By so doing they would be learning a good deal about the Christian faith as well as the process of relating it to life. From my point of view, that would be quality church education for youth. Admittedly, such a program would demand some imaginative, knowledgeable adults who can relate to youth. If congregations lack that kind of educational leadership, they had better train some.

Opportunities are needed to bring youth's concerns and the world's social problems into conversation with the Christian faith so that youth might discover its implications for action. There are many simple ways to facilitate such a learning process.

For example, I can remember meeting for supper with high school students in small groups in a local hangout. A group of twelve agreed to gather for a series of meetings. They committed themselves to addressing school issues, reflecting on what the Christian faith had to say about these issues, and to taking specific action on the issue in the light of that reflection. Each session began the same: "What issue concerns you today?" In each case our aim was to relate the Christian faith to the issue by moving from reflection into action and from action back to reflection. These two-hour weekly discussions grew increasingly popular. Their relevance was unquestioned. They helped me and the youth who joined me discover numerous ways to bring experience, identification, interpretation, action and reflection together in meaningful ways. While the old classroom, course, teacher-pupil relationship disappeared, learning increased. The Christian faith cannot be studied in a vacuum. Young people need to see models—exemplary life styles—of Christians acting and reflecting. They need to share experiences of relating the Christian faith to daily life.[3]

But again we must recognize that to facilitate any such education, adult education is crucial. By now it must be obvious that we should begin our total planning for a viable alternative future for church education with adults. Unless we do, it is doubtful if we will be able to bring into existence any of the models described in this chapter.

X. WHERE ELSE?

One issue remains. It is as broad as the total environment in which we live and all the forces of influence that are part of it. It includes our neighborhood and community, our government, the mass media, our schools, the arts, and all the other forces which influence and affect persons. Insofar as any of these inhibits human beings or enables them to be fully human individuals in community, we need to be concerned. Not only because we are Christians, but primarily because we claim to be church educators. An educator cannot confine himself to what goes on formally in educational institutions. Meaningful church education must make contact with those cultural forces which often have the strongest effect on the values and action-commitments of persons.

THE COMMUNITY

Just as the family plays a significant role in the nurturing of children, so does the local community. With the profound changes taking place in the American family, the society becomes more important. A child learns behavioral expectations and values in his community.

A number of years ago, a book entitled *The Short-changed Children of Suburbia* appeared.[1] It is a study of a town not far from New York City, but it could be any American suburb. From all outward appearances it is a model place to live and raise children. On closer examination, however, we discover something crucially important is missing. It lacks the possibility of dealing with human differences. To live responsibly in the world, we must learn to understand, respect, and seek the good of people who are different from ourselves as well as those like us. Too many suburbs set their inhabitants apart from the "outside" world. They are encompassed by sameness. This study implied that it is not healthy to live in a suburban or small town "ghetto." Learning to live responsibly in a pluralistic society is difficult when we live in a community of people too much like ourselves. Even more, the very sameness of such communities breeds destructive competition for bigger cars and more impressive television sets so that we can be just slightly ahead of our neighbor—that is, a little better in the same things among the same people. Inevitably there is a deadening inbreeding of interests and goals as well as an artificially limited horizon which engenders the belief that making everyone the same is the best of all states. Needless to say, as an educating community the church cannot ignore the character of the community and nation in which it exists.

Not long ago I sat in the kitchen of a sheep rancher in the vast openness of Wyoming's grazing land. Miles separated him from his nearest neighbor. As we talked through the night I found he was bothered by his environment. His thoughts went something like this:

"I love it here, but I can't expect my children to stay. There isn't much to do if you don't want to raise sheep. Nine out of ten of our high school graduates leave and go to work in some big city or attend college and then move near a city. You know, we don't prepare them for that. Out here on the range individualism is a good thing. Picking yourself up by your bootstraps works; it makes you strong enough to live on the range. An independent spirit is essential. There are a lot of qualities like those which are healthy if you want to live here. But I guess many of the opposite characteristics are needed to live responsibly in a city. It doesn't seem that people in the city can—even if they wanted to—pick themselves up by their bootstraps. In a city people become highly dependent on each other; they need to work as a team to solve their problems. I would guess that most of our children who move there vote against many pieces of legislation which are needed to deal with city problems. What am I going to do? What is our church out here on the range going to do to prepare them to live in a city?"

That was his story. He was interested in the environment in which he and his family live, as well as the environment in which the masses of Americans live and he saw these as an educational concern of his church. On that he was one hundred percent correct.

NATIONAL DECISION MAKING

Between our local community and the world lies our nation. It too plays a central role in the lives of people. The shape of our national life, its priorities, its programs, its laws, all these influence our values and action-commitments.

Each of us needs the assurance that we can make a difference in the world. Unless we possess the capacity to act in shaping our personal and social life, our integrity as persons is compromised. Many of us have a sense of futility regarding our ability to share in the decisions by which our common life is shaped. There appears to be a continuing growth of governmental forces that impinge upon our lives, denying us genuine options. The inherited mechanisms of public consent seem more and more inadequate to handle the situation. The same powerlessness is shared to a greater degree by blacks, Mexican-Americans, youth and the poor. We all need to learn ways by which we can speak and act with power about those decisions which affect our lives. Church education cannot ignore this issue. Church education needs both to be aware of the environment in which people live and how it affects them. Church education should help us develop the skills, values, commitments and incentives necessary to change our environment so that everyone can grow as a person of love, power and justice.

The community of faith, therefore, should educate its people for responsible decision making and citizenship. To do so is to help persons gain power and a sense of responsibility so that they can help create a society which will allow all persons to become fully human.

The Mass Media

The impact of television on man and society is infinite, its ramifications are only beginning to emerge. The mass media play an even more significant role in education. Children spend more time watching television than in almost any other single activity. Most television shows teach us something, and learning from television is more vivid and less time consuming than reading. Its influence is far greater than we can imagine. Television has tremendous educational possibilities. Most of us learn more through sight than words. So more quickly, comprehensively, and profoundly, television can transform us and the world in which we live. The question for church education is, How can we become knowledgeable enough to help direct and shape that power? Most of us may not be able to do that, but we can include television as it now exists within our educational concerns.

As a guest one evening of a television network executive, I observed that he had only one portable TV set which no one was watching. When I mentioned this fact he said, "My wife and I control the television in our home. Parents have to assume responsibility for what their children watch. There is a great deal on TV which I think is valuable and crucial for their education, and there are other programs which are either a waste of time or perhaps even detrimental. I wish people would make some value judgments and let us know what they want." We can affect the media. That is one of our responsibilities.

But church education cannot ignore the effects of mass media either—especially television. It will become increasingly important in the future. Reading Marshall McLuhan's book *Understanding Media* and Caleb Gattegno's *Towards a Visual Culture* [2] ought to convince us of that. If it doesn't, just look at the "new generation." Television has sensitized a whole generation of youth by making them emotionally and intellectually aware of the problems which face our world.

But youth often received that sensitization in "very passive ways"—by sitting and watching. While so doing, they had a minimum of experiences in which they could learn to live with others. Add to that our adult inability to find ways in which they might have a voice in our organizational structures or in the decisions which affect their lives and we have a serious problem. We have done little in church education to help them learn how to effect change in society constructively.

Is it any wonder that we have a generation which is highly sensitive to world problems and a drive to act out their concern, but which has not learned those skills necessary to effect the changes without violence? Unless church education helps persons to deal with their new awarenesses and equips them to change society for the good of all men, it has ignored one of its major responsibilities.

THE ARTS

No one should have to point out the importance of the arts and the educational role they play in society. Our culture—music, art, philosophy, literature, dance, drama—came out of the churches and monasteries. Once again the church is beginning to see the arts as important to its life. However, few of us as educators have taken them as seriously as we should. The arts continue to be a major educational force in society. We need to make them integral to the church's educational ministry.

In the Middle Ages, church architecture and the arts assumed the role of educator. The Mass became the primary place for learning. Each Sunday, the church presented the divine epic of God's action to save men. Each festival became a drama and the chancel a stage on which the community of faith re-enacted the biblical narrative. The medieval miracle and mystery plays put biblical stories into language familiar even to the illiterate. The morality play was more purposefully designed to educate as wandering churchmen dramatized allegories as a means of moral instruction. The lives of the saints served educational goals, as did pilgrimages and the Crusades.

In the Middle Ages, a layman's religion was dominated

by his sacramental life in the drama of the church year. Here, he was nurtured in the faith. The layman was introduced to the faith through participation in the life of the church. He learned informally through the stained glass and other art in churches. Monks copied and illuminated manuscripts and painted pictures.

People sought to understand the faith by making pilgrimages to holy places. They absorbed the meaning of the faith through their own participation in the arts.

Today new liturgies, songs, and contemporary forms of celebration are once again being created in the church. Church educators ought to take the lead in such developments as well as consider the educational implications of the arts in society. Drama is again moving into the streets. Actors protest the cruelties of war, poverty and racism by putting their shows on the street where their dramatic presentation cannot be ignored. I recall watching one on Fifth Avenue in New York City. Long stick puppets painted yellow, gowned in burlap and bound with ropes represented a Christ figure and his disciples. They were carried in single file behind effigies of the President and Uncle Sam. Behind the disciples marched soldier puppets in gray followed by a division of skeleton-like heads singing the Marine Battle Hymn. Along with these giant stick puppets came persons in gray gowns symbolizing women in mourning. They held their "dead babies" at arm's length. The feeling provoked by their performance was so intense that both the Christ figure and Uncle Sam were attacked and disfigured by the onlookers.

Today the demonstrations and the "march" have become dramatic acts of education. Posters, buttons and signs join them as modern artistic expressions whose aim is to teach. Music and folk singing become major learning experiences for the new generation. Not only ought the church educator to become part of their expression in the world, but he needs to encourage them to become integral to the educational life of the church.

THE PUBLIC SCHOOLS

One last learning environment needs to be mentioned. Perhaps it is the most important for church educators. It is the public schools. So many people are so much involved in schools for so large a portion of their lives that Christian educators ought to turn critical and constructive attention upon them.

Education should prepare persons for citizenship, yet often public education is exclusively centered on the pursuit of private pleasure and personal objectives at the expense of public responsibility.

Education should equip persons to understand and function effectively within a world of diverse cultures, languages and political commitments. Persons emerge from high school—urban, suburban, or rural—unappreciative of other cultures, and generally suspicious of and derogatory toward the rest of the world.

Education should encourage self-reliance, self-determination, creativity, individuality, imagination, and diversity; schools often create submissive, conformist, and dependent students.

Education should provide the impetus for innovation and change in society by teaching that striving for basic changes and reformation in the practices and structures of society is a continuously necessary and proper task. Yet often schools are strongly oriented to what *is* rather than producing commitment to reform in a continuing search for a more just society. Although we insist that the advantages of education should be freely available to all persons and groups, there are great class and racial disparities in the educational opportunities offered the citizens of the United States.

Education should be adequately supported by public funds since it is basic to the continued existence and health of a democratic society. The American public, on the contrary, seems to prefer to allocate the nation's wealth to the purchase of private consumer goods and services. Perhaps the church as an educating community needs to take the lead in creating schools where the kind of education they believe in can exist. As a matter of fact, some have.

One day, fifteen youth and three adults met to discuss education in their community. They wanted a school where they could apply what they were learning, an action center where things happen, a place where they could experiment and learn what they wanted to know, a place where they could deal with the issues that faced them and their community. It was their conviction that the public schools not only neglected these concerns but were turning kids off. They saw little need for grades, classroom structure, typical teacher/pupil relationships.

The result: their own "school" or as they prefer "experience center." The policy and direction of the BEAM (Burlington Ecumenical Action Ministry) school are decided by all those who attend it. As one of their first acts the group chose two recent college graduates as their adult leaders. Their aim is to help each individual learn to relate to himself and his community as a supplement to the academic learning acquired in the public schools. The BEAM school is for everyone no matter what his age. There are no teachers or pupils in the usual sense, only learners.

It is encouraging to see persons who are desperate for a humane school environment banding together and starting little schools of their own. We need more! *The Lives of Children,* by George Dennison, is must reading for anyone truly interested in bringing one to life.[3] Dennison is representative of all those who have a plan for changing public education in America. Church educators should be among them.

According to Thomas Green of Syracuse University, "The central question is not 'dare the schools build a new social order?' They probably will not; they probably cannot; and indeed, they probably never could. The significant question is 'Dare the society build a new system of schools?' The answer to that question is problematic but it is at least the right question." It is one with which the church as an educating community ought to deal.

A FINAL NOTE

It may appear as if I have placed a tremendously heavy responsibility on the church educator. I have! You may wonder whether everything we have discussed can possibly be accomplished. I think it can. We may have to stop some of the things we've been doing in our churches and establish some new priorities. That isn't out of the realm of the possible, if we think it important.

Like Max Lerner, I characterize myself as neither an optimist nor a pessimist, but rather a possiblist. Life is a great possibility, realizable through hope and organized, planned human activity. A birth of new vitality and relevance in religious education can break forth. It can also abort. The decision is ours. So is the responsibility. At stake are tomorrow's children. Nothing more, nothing less.

Notes

I. THE OPEN PRESENT

1. Daniel Bell, "The Trajectory of an Idea," *Daedalus*, Journal of the American Academy of Arts and Sciences, Boston, Mass., Vol. 96, No. 3, Summer 1967, p. 639. Used by permission.
2. Ellis Nelson, *Where Faith Begins* (Richmond: John Knox Press, 1967), p. 10.
3. Krister Stendahl, "Religion, Mysticism, and the Institutional Church," *Daedalus*, op. cit., p. 857.

II. WHERE WE WERE

1. Walter Scott Athearn, *Religious Education and American Democracy* (Boston: Pilgrim Press, 1917), pp. 60 f.
2. Robert Lynn, *Protestant Strategies in Education* (New York: Association Press, 1964), pp. 25 f.
3. Ibid., p. 53.

IV. ACT IT OUT!

1. Norbert Wiener, *Ex Prodigy* (Cambridge, Mass.: M.I.T. Press, 1953), p. 9.
2. Reinhold Niebuhr, "Death of a Martyr." Reprinted from the June 25, 1945 issue of *Christianity and Crisis*, copyright © 1945 by Christianity and Crisis, Inc.
3. Wilfred Cantwell Smith, *Questions of Religious Truth* (New York: Charles Scribner's Sons, 1967), pp. 110 f.

V. THE RIGHT START

1. G. Ernest Wright, *The Rule of God* (New York: Doubleday, 1960), p. 41.

VI. DOWN WITH SCHOOL!

1. Quoted by Origen, *Contra Celsum III*, p. 5.

VII. WHERE WE ARE NOW

1. Ellis Nelson, *Where Faith Begins* (Richmond: John Knox Press, 1967), p. 203.

VIII. NEVER TOO EARLY

1. Benjamin Bloom, *Stability and Change in Human Characteristics* (New York: John Wiley & Sons, 1964).

2. *Colloquy,* Jan. 1968.

3. Gabriel Moran, *Vision and Tactics: Toward an Adult Church* (New York: Herder & Herder, 1968).

IX. ALTERNATIVES

1. For a more accurate, detailed description and evaluation of this model see "Alternatives," *Colloquy,* Oct. 1970, pp. 45 f.

2. George Leonard, *Education and Ecstasy* (New York: Dell, 1968).

3. For a detailed description of a new youth education action/reflection model I recommend "Politicizing Youth," *Colloquy,* June 1970, pp. 30–37. This model is one of the best I know.

X. WHERE ELSE?

1. Alice Miel, *The Short-changed Children of Suburbia* (New York: Institute of Human Relations Press, 1967).

2. Marshall McLuhan, *Understanding Media* (New York: McGraw-Hill, 1964).

Caleb Gattegno, *Towards a Visual Culture* (New York: Outerbridge and Dienstrey, 1969).

3. George Dennison, *The Lives of Children* (New York: Random House, 1969).